THE MARSHALL CAVENDISH ✩ ✩ ✩ ILLUSTRATED ✩ ✩ ✩ ENCYCLOPEDIA OF WORLD WAR II

WORLD WAR II

VOLUME 15

THE MARSHALL CAVENDISH ☆ ☆ ☆ ILLUSTRATED ☆ ☆ ☆ ENCYCLOPEDIA OF

WORLD WAR II

Based on the original text by
Lieutenant Colonel Eddy Bauer

CONSULTANT EDITOR

Brigadier General James L. Collins, Jr., U.S.A.

CHIEF OF MILITARY HISTORY,
DEPARTMENT OF THE ARMY

MARSHALL CAVENDISH CORPORATION/NEW YORK

CONTENTS

Editorial Director: Brian Innes
Editor-in-chief; Brigadier Peter Young, D.S.O., M.C., M.A.
Managing Editor: Richard Humble
Editor: Christopher Chant
Art Editor: Jim Bridge

Airborne war: learning the trade

1. *The first use of airborne troops in World War II: a German paratrooper collapses the canopy of his parachute after landing in Norway during the invasion of April 1940. The daring, and in the event successful, use of such airborne forces in the invasion of Denmark and Norway should have warned the Allies of what could happen in the West–such as the audacious glider landing on Eben-Emaël.*

Airborne re-supply to troops in the field was successfully attempted at the end of World War I, but it was the Russians who pioneered paratroop training in the early 1930's.

The foreign observers at the manoeuvres near Kiev in 1936 saw two battalions with light weapons land in eight minutes and occupy the town which was their objective. There was some interest and experiments by the western countries, but only the Germans and Italians considered vertical envelopment as a valuable tactic.

The German paratroops were trained by the Luftwaffe, and from the beginning were picked troops. In 1940 they saw action in Denmark and Norway, where they were involved in heavy fighting. In the West, a team of airborne sappers neutralised the Belgian fort of Eben-Emaël, and paratroops attacked airfields and bridges in Holland.

The following year paratroops seized the bridge over the Corinth canal, a vital bottleneck in the British escape route from Greece. It was on the island of Crete, however, that on May 20, 1941 the *Fallschirmjäger* achieved their greatest success. Despite heavy losses they secured Maleme airfield and Ju 52's started to fly in Major-General Julius Ringel's

1

German paratroopers in training, from a German history of airborne forces published in 1940.

2. *Trainees learn how to fall after reaching the ground. The failure to do this properly usually meant at least a sprained ankle if not a broken one. Note the parachutes hanging up behind the trainees.*
3. *Getting the feeling of swinging under the canopy.*
4. *A German paratrooper in full jumping kit. In his left hand he is holding the static line, which was clipped to a wire in the aircraft before the jump. As the man left the aircraft, the static line pulled open the pack, allowing the parachute to blossom out once the jumper was clear of the aircraft.*
5. *The German paratrooper's badge, a diving eagle in a wreath of oak and laurel.*
6. *The paratrooper's cuff title, silver thread on green: "Fallschirm-Jäger-Rgt." (Parachute Regiment).*

mountain division. Attacked by fresh troops with heavy weapons, the British were doomed and by May 27 the island was firmly occupied. The losses from Operation "Mercury" were very heavy, the paratroops and assault troops losing 3,250 killed and 3,400 wounded, with about 100 Ju 52's destroyed. Though they were used as élite ground troops throughout the war, the *Fallschirmjäger* made only limited drops at Catania in Sicily in July 1943, at Leros later that year, and a final disorganised jump during the Ardennes offensive in December 1944.

The Russians made only one operational landing during the war. This little-documented attack, on September 24, 1943, was made in support of an assault crossing of the Dniepr loop between Kiev and Kanev. The operation was a disaster as many aircraft were lost or shot down, and the troops scattered. But the chief reason for the failure was that the dropping zone was in the path of 10th *Panzergrenadier* Division and other units moving up to the front.

The Japanese employed paratroops in their attacks on the Dutch East Indies in 1942 and other island hopping operations, but they served more for infiltration than exploitation.

The British and Americans were not slow to learn from the German successes, and at Ring-way in Great Britain and Fort Benning in the U.S.A. the Allies began training and developing drills for mass parachute drops.

The first British operation was on February 10, 1941, when 38 men were dropped to attack the Tragino Aqueduct in southern Italy. Though the target was attacked, the damage was negligible and soon repaired.

On February 27 and 28, 1942, the Parachute Regiment won its first battle honour in the Bruneval Raid. Operation "Biting" was carried out by "C" Company, 2nd Parachute Battalion. At the cost of three killed and six missing the raid on the French coast secured a German radar set.

At the end of the year, British paratroops captured Bône airfield, Tunisia, in their first battalion-strength operation.

In July 1943 the 1st Air Landing Brigade and the 1st Parachute Brigade were in action in Sicily capturing the Ponte Grande Bridge and the Primosole Bridge.

D-Day saw the 6th Airborne Division covering the left flank of the Allied landings. In this rôle it captured the Merville Battery and the Pegasus Bridge.

Meanwhile in the south, the 2nd Independent Brigade Group made up part of the 1st Airborne Task Force in the landings of Operation "Dragoon" on August 15.

At the end of 1944, as the Allies thrust through France and Bel-

gium to the borders of Germany, General Montgomery launched Operation "Market Garden", and the 1st Airborne Division jumped over Arnhem.

The American experience was similar to that of the British. In the early 1930's there were theoretical discussions, but it was the successful employment of paratroops in war that started practical training. Lieutenant-

4

5

7

8

10

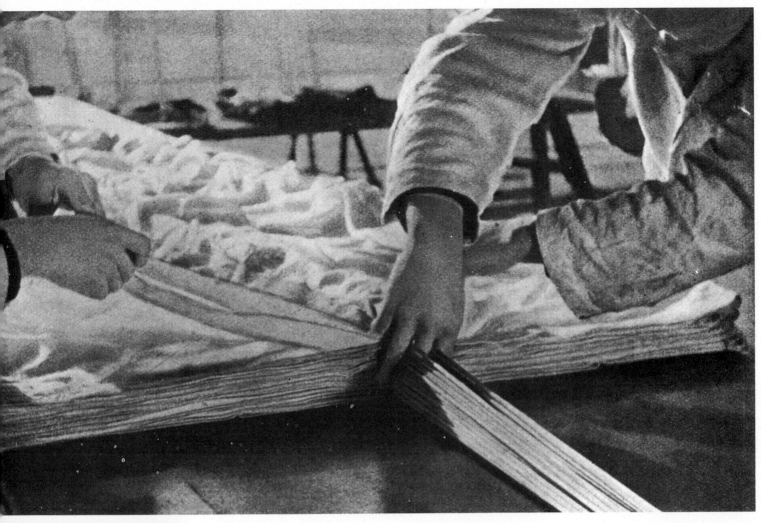

Colonel William C. Lee, who commanded the Provisional Parachute Group at Fort Benning, Georgia, pioneered the training.

Like the British, U.S. paratroops had a distinctive uniform and extra pay, but they also suffered from a similar lack of equipment and insufficient aircraft.

U.S. paratroops went into action at Oran and Youks-les-Bains in North Africa during the "Torch" landings. These operations, and a demolition raid on El Djem in Tunisia, showed that sufficient time for detailed planning was essential.

Tragically, Sicily again proved that planning was inadequate. In two drops soldiers were so scattered that only one-eighth landed in front of the 1st Division beaches at Gela. The plan to drop the 504th Regimental Combat Team to reinforce the 82nd Airborne Division at Gela suffered badly after the transports came under fire from the invasion fleet: 23 aircraft were shot down, among them six with troops still on board. As the paratroops jumped they came under Allied fire, and some were even fired at after they had reached the ground.

However, though the Allies were dissappointed with the attacks in Sicily, the Germans considered them a success. The scattered soldiers dislocated the enemy rear, and Italian prisoners estimated the number of American paratroops as between 20,000 and 30,000, whereas only about 5,000 men were involved.

The airborne assault on Normandy by the 82nd and the 101st Airborne Divisions was again scattered, but this worked to the Americans' advantage. With no battalion concentrations there was no target to counter-attack, and German patrols sent out to mop up the enemy found themselves involved in hundreds of local fire-fights.

In southern France the Americans achieved their most accurate mass combat drop to date. Nearly 60 per cent of the troops landed on the three assigned drop zones in Operation "Dragoon". But when the 3rd Division approached St. Tropez, one of its objectives, it found that airborne troops had already occupied the area and captured the garrison of 240 Germans, an anti-aircraft battery,

7. *Part of a stick of German paratroopers leaves its Junkers Ju 52 transport aircraft. Note the weapons container on the extreme left. Until they could reach this, when they landed the paratroops would be entirely dependent on personal weapons.*
8. *Before emplaning. The special helmet was a cut-down version of the standard German helmet.*
9. *The delicate work of parachute packing. Unless the canopy was folded correctly and the rigging lines kept untangled, there was every possibility of the parachute twisting up, or "Roman candling", causing the paratrooper to plummet to his death.*
10. *Practice in leaving the aircraft.*

11. *After ground training and short drops from a practice tower, British paratroopers next moved on to drops from a static balloon. Note the basket, with a circular hatch to simulate that on the underneath of the converted bombers used as Great Britain's first paratroop-dropping aircraft.*

12. *A drop from an Armstrong-Whitworth Whitley II of the 1st Parachute Training School.*

14

13. *British paratroopers make a last careful inspection of their own and their comrades' kit before emplaning. Note the special smock and helmets. The aircraft in the background is a Whitley.*

14. *Ready to go. Note the quick release device on the harness (turn to unlock and press to release) and the Sten sub-machine gun carried by the man second from the left.*

After the success of German
parachute troops in 1940, the
United States and Great Britain
began to train airborne forces.
In America, a school was
established at Hightstown, New
Jersey, under Major-General
George A. Lynch, where an
initial cadre of 48 men was
trained to serve as instructors.
15. A novice begins his training
with a jump from a 125-foot
practice tower.
16. A year later, in June 1941,
the practice tower had been
improved, and training had
intensified as the war in Europe
expanded.

1969

17. *A final check as each man clips his static line before the jump.*
18. *Under the concerned eyes of an R.A.F. dispatcher, a Colour Sergeant prepares to jump.*
19. *A paratrooper in mid exit as he hits the slipstream of the aircraft.*
20. *In near perfect conditions the stick reforms after the jump. Even a slight wind could scatter the men and weapons containers over a wide area and prevent the formation of an effective force.*

and two coastal batteries – the airborne troops were those from 20 planes who had jumped prematurely on the red signal light.

The day-light drop by the U.S. 82nd and 101st Airborne Divisions in Operation "Market Garden" proved, contrary to the grim predictions of some planners, to be a spectacular success. Men of the 101st seized their objectives, though one bridge was found to be destroyed. The Guards Armoured Division built a replacement and pressed on towards the 82nd, holding Grave and the ground south-east of Nijmegen. The 82nd had been driven back from the bridge over the Waal. In a joint attack the U.S. 504th Parachute Regiment and the Guards captured the Nijmegen bridge.

For the Americans the operation showed that a day-light drop gave a greater concentration, and could be achieved at low cost, providing there was complete air superiority and sufficient aircraft to fly *Flak* suppression missions.

In the Far East, the Chindit operations in Burma during 1944 further demonstrated what could be achieved with air superiority.

With gliders and transport aircraft, the British placed the 3rd Indian Division behind the Japanese lines. The troops were supplied with stores to build a series of "strongholds" as a base for operations against the Japanese lines of communication. Light aircraft were used for liaison and to evacuate wounded from the airstrips constructed near the strongholds. When the Japanese at last diverted men from the front to attack the strongholds, they lost between 1,500 and 2,000 men in attacks against "White City", the stronghold which earned the reputation of the "most efficient Japanese-killer of the whole Burma campaign".

Yet paratroops and an air-landing capacity were an arm which, with the exception of selected raids on local targets, and the operations in Burma and Crete, were used as an expensive luxury by planners and ground commanders. For, however, impressive airborne operations may appear, many of the objectives secured by vertical envelopment could have been reached by conventional forces.

CHAPTER 132

ARNHEM: Monty's gamble fails

General Bradley has described his stupefaction on learning of Operation "Market Garden" which Montgomery had got Eisenhower to approve and with which Bradley did not agree:

"Had the pious teetotaling Montgomery wobbled into S.H.A.E.F. with a hangover, I could not have been more astonished than I was by the daring adventure he proposed. For in contrast to the conservative tactics Montgomery ordinarily chose, the Arnhem attack was to be made over a 60-mile carpet of airborne troops. Although I never reconciled myself to the venture, I nevertheless freely concede that Monty's plan for Arnhem was one of the most imaginative of the war."

In effect the "carpet" over which XXX Corps was to advance towards the northern outskirts of Arnhem was 60 miles long and criss-crossed six times by canals and watercourses. Eisenhower had put at Montgomery's disposal the 1st Airborne Army. Commanded by U.S. Lieutenant-General L. H. Brereton, it engaged its I Airborne Corps (Lieutenant-General F. A. M. Browning) as follows:

1. U.S. 101st Airborne Division (Major-General Maxwell D. Taylor) would take Eindhoven by surprise and seize the bridges on the Wilhelmina Canal, the Dommel, and the Willems Canal;

2. U.S. 82nd Airborne Division (Major-General James M. Gavin) would take the Grave bridge over the Maas and the Nijmegen bridge over the Waal (the southern arm of the Rhine); and

3. British 1st Airborne Division (Major-General R. E. Urquhart) would take the bridges over the Neder Rijn (the

△ *Part of the human cargo of an Airspeed Horsa glider waits in the sunshine on an airfield in England before the start of operation "Market Garden". Gliders offered the advantage of putting down a platoon of men in one spot, whereas paratroops could be scattered and take time to form into an effective force.*
◁ *The skies over Arnhem fill with parachutes in the opening stages of the operation.*

Operation "Market Garden"

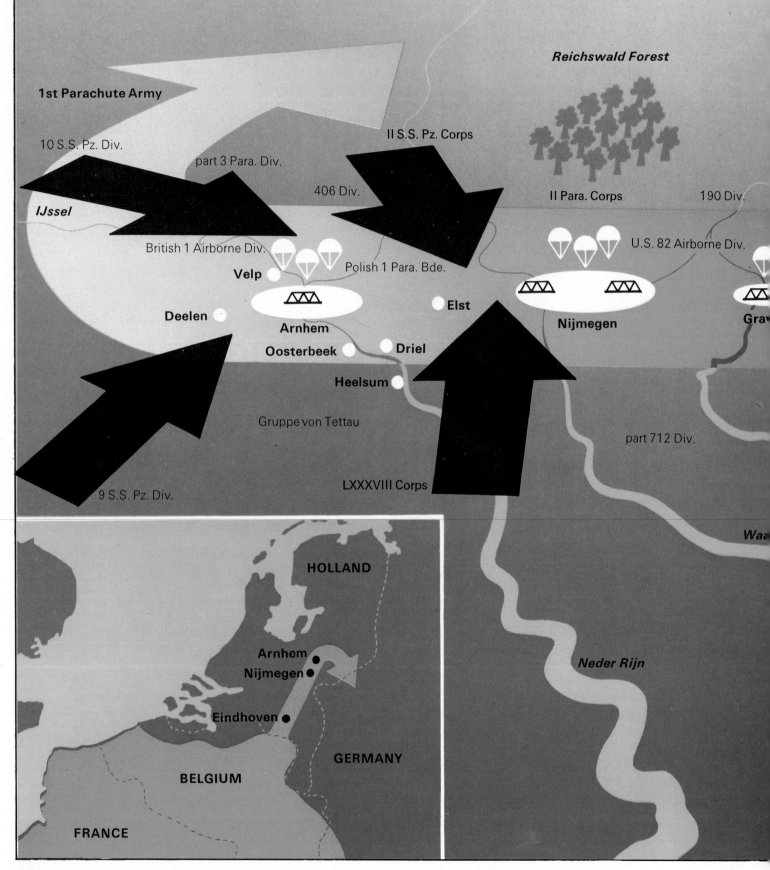

Reichswald Forest

1st Parachute Army

10 S.S. Pz. Div.

II S.S. Pz. Corps

part 3 Para. Div.

406 Div.

II Para. Corps

190 Div.

IJssel

British 1 Airborne Div.

Polish 1 Para. Bde.

U.S. 82 Airborne Div.

Velp

Deelen

Elst

Nijmegen

Gra

Arnhem

Oosterbeek

Driel

Heelsum

Gruppe von Tettau

part 712 Div.

LXXXVIII Corps

9 S.S. Pz. Div.

Waa

HOLLAND

Arnhem

Nijmegen

Neder Rijn

Eindhoven

GERMANY

BELGIUM

FRANCE

1974

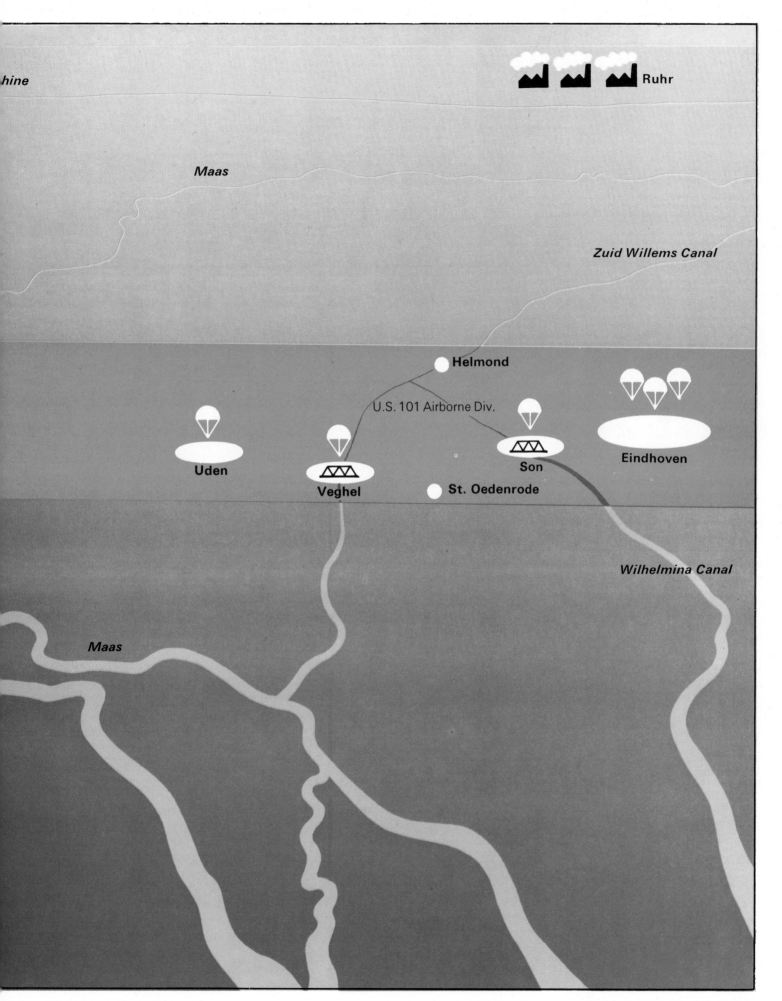

hine

Ruhr

Maas

Zuid Willems Canal

Helmond

U.S. 101 Airborne Div.

Uden

Veghel

St. Oedenrode

Son

Eindhoven

Maas

Wilhelmina Canal

1975

△ △ *Two film cameramen, part of the team that gave extensive press coverage to the operation. They were to record the struggle in some of the most vivid film and photographs of the war.*

△ *Two paratroopers of the 82nd Airborne Division check their kit before emplaning. The 82nd Airborne jumped at Nijmegen and captured bridges over the Maas and Maas-Waal canal, but failed to reach the Nijmegen bridges. These were later taken in a joint assault with XXX Corps.*

▷ *The interior of a Dakota; the soldiers carry their weapons, with their kit packed in leg bags, or worn under their smocks to prevent it catching in the parachute harness.*

northern arm of the Rhine) at Arnhem. It would then establish a bridgehead around the town and be reinforced by the Polish 1st Parachute Brigade, then by the British 52nd (Airportable) Division.

It was along the corridor opened up by these forces that the three divisions of the British XXX Corps (the Guards Armoured, the 43rd, and the 50th Divisions) under Horrocks were to advance towards Arnhem and, breaking out of the bridgehead, drive on at full speed to the Zuiderzee, a final run of about 37 miles.

Allied Intelligence misses II Panzer Corps

All things considered, it does seem that Operation "Market Garden" relied heavily on what Frederick the Great called "Her Sacred Majesty Chance" and the expectation that she would favour Generals Browning and Horrocks for several days and under all circumstances. Even had she favoured them throughout, however, it is unlikely that XXX Corps could have made the run to Berlin all alone, as Eisenhower had no strategic reserves or logistic resources to exploit fully any initial success of this risky enterprise.

It must be admitted that by getting his chief to ratify his plan, Field-Marshal Montgomery thought that only a motley of decimated, disarmed, and demoralised divisions separated him from final victory, and that because of this he could outstep the bounds of prudence, or even that prudence demanded him to be bold. Otherwise the enemy would get his breath and his courage back. In this he was wrong, but the mistake in this appreciation must be attributed to shortcomings in the Intelligence services of

The British Airspeed Horsa I assault glider

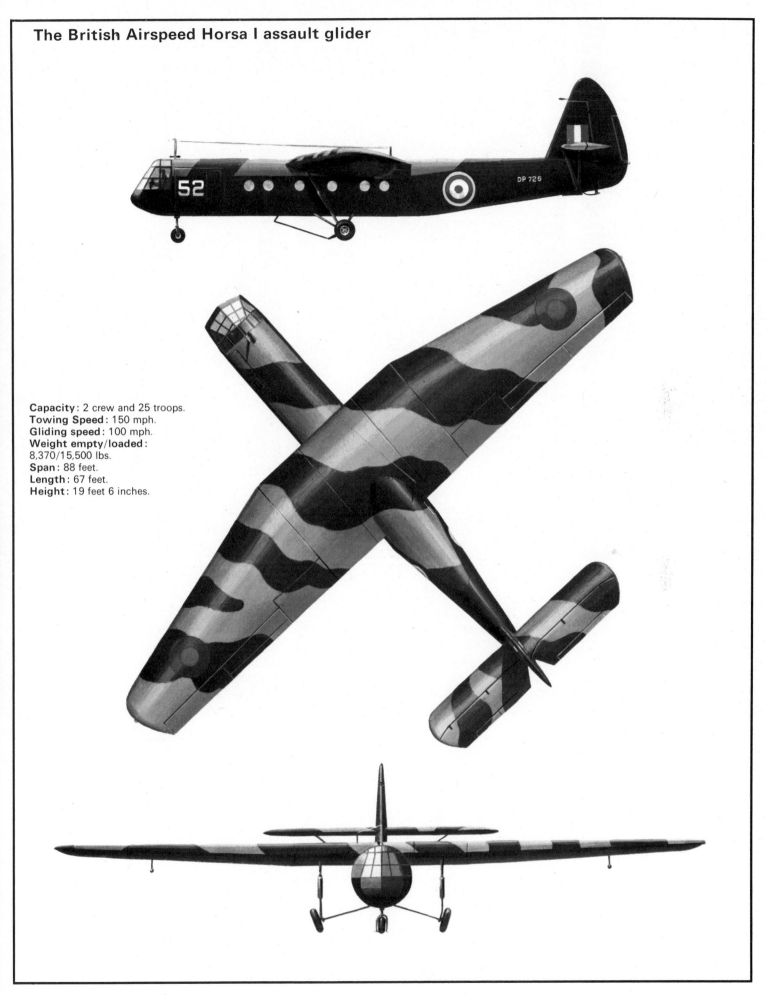

Capacity: 2 crew and 25 troops.
Towing Speed: 150 mph.
Gliding speed: 100 mph.
Weight empty/loaded:
8,370/15,500 lbs.
Span: 88 feet.
Length: 67 feet.
Height: 19 feet 6 inches.

△ *Parachutes litter the ground on a dropping zone outside Arnhem.*
▷ △ *Men of the headquarters group of the 1st Airborne Division's artillery start unloading from the first two Horsas to land.*
▷ *The fatal delay. Between four and six hours elapsed before the troops could arrive at the bridge. Some were slowed down by enthusiastic Dutch civilians, who greeted them as liberators.*
▷ ▷ *Landing Zone "Z" covered with gliders, some of which have been broken in half for unloading.*

21st Army Group and S.H.A.E.F.

In particular, it seems to have escaped them that in the region of 's Hertogenbosch a new German army (the 1st Parachute), with six or seven divisions, was in the making under the command of Colonel-General Kurt Student, the victor of Crete. Allied aircraft, it is true, had noticed a definite increase in flak in the Arnhem area as they flew over on their way to bomb the Ruhr, but no one guessed that this was to cover the assembly of II S.S. Panzer Corps, hastily recouping its losses after Falaise.

Clearly in this period of intense movement the Intelligence services were having a difficult time of it. But Operation "Market Garden" produced one surprise after another. Bradley registered his forthright objection once he had been let into Montgomery's confidence:

". . . as soon as I learned of Monty's plan, I telephoned Ike and objected strenuously to it. For in abandoning the joint offensive, Monty would slip off on a tangent and leave us holding the bag. But Ike silenced my objections; he thought the plan a fair gamble. It might enable us to outflank the Siegfried Line, perhaps even snatch a Rhine bridgehead."

Events were to prove Bradley all too right.

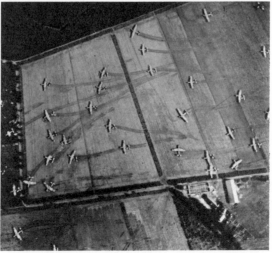

Page 1981: *Action and reaction. As the British forces moved in to Arnhem, the Germans under Field-Marshal Model set up a defensive perimeter and raced to hold the bridges. Allied Intelligence had underestimated the strength of the forces available in the area.*
△ *A Sturmgeschütz III with a re-supply parachute in the foreground.*
▷ *Paratroops with a Jeep-towed 6-pdr anti-tank gun.*

The American Douglas C-47 Skytrain transport and glider tug

Engines: two Pratt & Whitney R-1830
Twin Wasp radials, 1,200-hp each.
Speed: 230 mph at 8,800 feet.
Ceiling: 24,100 feet.
Range: 2,125 miles.
Weight empty/loaded:
16,865/31,000 lbs.
Capacity: 7,500 lbs, 28 troops, or a
towed glider.
Span: 95 feet.
Length: 64 feet 6 inches.
Height: 16 feet 11 inches.
Crew: 4.

Operation "Market Garden"

On Sunday September 17, 1944, zero hour struck at 1430. Under the near or distant cover of 1,200 fighters the first elements of Lieutenant-General Browning's three airborne divisions, which had been packed into 2,800 aircraft and 1,600 gliders, jumped or landed as close as possible to their objectives without undue losses.

For the 101st Airborne Division all went well, except for the Son bridge over the Wilhelmina Canal which it could not save from destruction. The 82nd managed to surprise the Grave bridge, but in the evening, when the Germans had got over the shock, it failed in its first attempt on Nijmegen. By this time General Student had got the plans for "Market Garden" which had been found on board an American glider shot down behind the German lines. Because of heavy A.A. fire round Arnhem it had been decided that the first echelon of the British 1st Airborne Division would drop in heath-land seven miles from the Neder Rijn bridges.

H.Q. Army Group "B" was at Oosterbeek, and here Field-Marshal Model watched the landing and nearly got put in the bag together with his general staff. He jumped into a car, alerted General Bittrich, commanding II S.S. Panzer Corps, and counter-attacked with the 9th *"Hohenstaufen"* Panzer Division through

△ *Major-General Urquhart, G.O.C. 1st Airborne Division, with the Pegasus pennant outside his H.Q. at the Hartenstein Hotel.*

▷ *House clearing in Oosterbeek. Each side used snipers, and while the British found that they had to be careful moving in the open, Sturmbannführer Sepp Kraft described the British tree and ground snipers as "the very devil".*

▽ ▷ *A casualty is brought into the Hartenstein Hotel. By the end of the nine days' fighting, only 3,000 of the 10,095 men who landed (including glider pilots) were capable of crossing to the Allied lines.*

▽ ▷ ▷ *Paratroopers adopt all-round defence at a cross roads. In the foreground is a P.I.A.T. anti-tank weapon. Supported by some glider-borne 6-pdr anti-tank guns, it was to be the chief weapon to combat the German tanks and assault guns. Despite its crude appearance, it was an effective weapon, though it had a powerful recoil. Its 3-lb projectile could pierce four inches of armour at short ranges.*

◁ The Arnhem road bridge. On the ramp at the northern end are the remains of a German armoured column destroyed by the 2nd Parachute Battalion under Lieutenant-Colonel Frost.

▽ A contrast in military élites. Prisoners from the 9th "Hohenstaufen" S.S. Panzer Division with their British captors.
▽▽ Men of the 1st Battalion, The Border Regiment await an attack at Oosterbeek.

△ *A 6-pdr anti-tank gun in ambush. The crew are about to fire on an assault gun which is only 80 yards away.*
▷ △ *A 75-mm pack howitzer of the 1st Airlanding Light Regiment in action. They were used as anti-tank weapons to supplement the 1st and 2nd Anti-Tank Batteries, but were a poor substitute with their low muzzle velocity and slow cross-axle traverse.*

Arnhem and the 10th *"Frundsberg"* along the left bank of the Neder Rijn.

The British outpaced

In this test of speed the British did not have the advantage as, for technical and topographical reasons, their radio communications broke down. This untoward event even caused Urquhart to go up to the front himself, and within minutes he had lost all means of co-ordinating the movements of his division. Towards 2000 hours Lieutenant-Colonel Frost's battalion, whose commander had led the raid on Bruneval in 1941, had reached a point opposite the road bridge at Arnhem, but was almost surrounded.

Supported on the left by XII Corps and on the right by VIII Corps (Lieutenant-General Evelyn H. Baring), XXX Corps got off to a good start. Admirably supported, as its commander said, by No. 83 Group, Tactical Air Force (Air Vice-Marshal H. Broadhurst), it reached Valkenswaard at the end of the day. A day later its Guards Armoured Division was at Son, where the bridge over the canal was repaired by dawn on the 19th. There was good contact with the 82nd Airborne Division, which had resumed its attack on Nijmegen, but without much success.

By now it had begun to rain. "Market Garden", in fact, enjoyed only one day of blue skies out of ten. Were the weather forecasts ignored? There were consequential delays in the reinforcement of the airborne divisions and a notable drop in efficiency of the ground support. XXX Corps had only one axis along which to advance its 23,000 vehicles. During the 19th, Horrocks was able to get his tanks from Son to Nijmegen (36 miles), but it was not until the evening of the following day that the British and the Americans, fighting side by side, succeeded in crossing the Waal and seizing the road and rail bridges which Model had ordered to be left intact for a counter-attack.

"When he had been given his orders in Monty's caravan the day before Browning asked how long he would be required to hold the bridge.

"'Two days' said Monty briskly. 'They'll be up with you by then.'

"'We can hold it for four' Browning replied. 'But I think we might be going a bridge too far.'"

The British driven back

The operation was now in its fifth day, and during the night of September 19-20 Urquhart had had to resign himself to abandoning Frost to his fate and to pulling his unit into the district of Oosterbeek with its back to the Neder Rijn. The bad weather continued, air supplies were

The German 3.7-cm *Flak* 36 (Sf) *auf Zugkraftwagen* 5t A.A. mounting

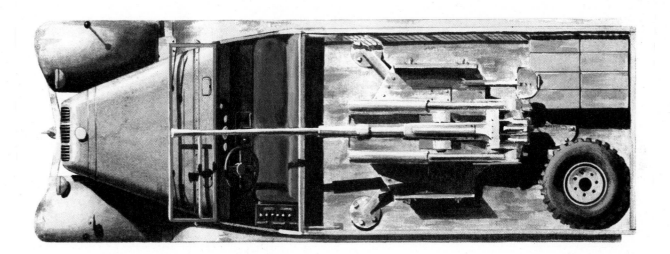

Weight: 10.4 tons.
Crew: 7.
Armament: one 3.7-cm *Flak* 36 L/98 gun.
Engine: one Maybach NL 38 TUKRM inline, 90-hp.
Speed: 25 mph.
Range: 150 miles.
Length: 19 feet 9 inches.
Width: 7 feet 3 inches.
Height: 8 feet 2 inches (vehicle).

reduced to practically nothing, and what was dropped fell equally amongst the Germans and the Allies. In the evening of the 21st, Lieutenant-Colonel Frost was seriously wounded and his battalion, now reduced to about 100 men, was captured by the Germans. On the 21st and 22nd the Polish 1st Parachute Brigade (Major-General Sosabowski) landed almost opposite Oosterbeek, whilst the Guards (Major-General Allan Adair) and the 43rd Division (Major-General Ivor Thomas) were caught in flank by the 10th *"Frundsberg"* S.S. Panzer Division as they tried to cover the ten miles between the Waal and the Neder Rijn. XXX Corps' forward positions, now sticking out like a finger in the German lines, risked being cut off at any moment from either east or west.

The survivors of the British 1st Airborne Division now received the order to pull back to the left bank of the Neder Rijn. 2,163 of them got across during the night of September 25-26 out of a total of 8,905 officers, N.C.O.s, and men and the 1,100 glider-pilots who had held off the attacks of II S.S. Panzer Corps for the last ten days. The Poles left behind 1,000 of their men and the U.S. 82nd and 101st Airborne Divisions lost respectively 1,669 and 2,074 killed, wounded, and missing. Between September 17 and 30, then, about one-third of the 34,876 men who fought between Eindhoven and Arnhem were lost. The people of Arnhem showed admirable devotion and courage in hiding 250 British paratroopers and helping them to escape: among these were Brigadiers J. W. Hackett and G. W. Lathbury.

Major-General Urquhart's epic at Arnhem

In a letter dated September 28 and written in his own hand, Field-Marshal Montgomery expressed the admiration he felt at the bearing of Major-General Urquhart's division. Recalling the centuries-old roll-call of famous deeds by British arms, he wrote to him:

"There can be few episodes more glorious than the epic of Arnhem, and those that follow after will find it hard to live up to the high standards that you have set.

"So long as we have in the armies of the British Empire officers and men who will do as you have done, then we can indeed look forward with complete confidence to the future. In years to come it will be a great thing for a man to be able to say 'I fought at Arnhem!'"

"Market Garden" a failure

History will bear out this judgement. It is not certain, however, that it will also ratify Montgomery's conclusions on the glorious and tragic episode. In his opinion, if the success of the undertaking was not as great as had been expected, this was because the supply services, contrary to Eisenhower's orders, refused to cut down on rations for the American 3rd Army. General Bradley thought otherwise and wrote to the C.-in-C. on September 21: ". . . all plans for the future operations always lead back to the fact that in order to supply an operation of any size beyond the Rhine, the port of Antwerp is essential."

On September 4 the Scheldt estuary could have been cleared within a few days, and the rapidity of this success would have been a real shot in the arm to the Allied supply problem. Instead, the operation started on September 29 by the 21st Army Group dragged on for a whole month. By November 3 it was all over, but the Germans had profited from the delay by mining the canal, and clearing operations took another three weeks of dangerous and intensive work. Antwerp's major port facilities thus went unused from September 4 to November 23, whilst less than 90 miles away to the south-west the U.S. 1st Army was reduced to cutting down on petrol and ammunition. There were, of course, the "Red Ball Highways". The American historian Robert W. Merrian, writing of these roads, organised from August 25 onwards by Lieutenant-General J. C. H. Lee, says of the service:

"The Red Ball supply high road grew and grew, like Topsy, until it stretched over 700 well-marked miles, thoroughly equipped with fast wreckage and servicing stations manned twenty-four hours a day. The Red Ball began operating on August 25 with 5,400 vehicles, hauled a daily average of about 5,000 tons of supplies for the eighty-one days of its operation. On its peak day of operation, over 12,000 tons of supplies were hauled to the front, more than enough for twelve fighting divisions. Operating on a circle route,

▷ U.S. paratroopers, caught in the open by German artillery fire, duck and sprint for cover.
▷ ▷ ▽ A 3-inch mortar crew in action. Note the two striped rods resting against the parapet of the weapons pit. These were used in aiming, and here they probably define the arc of fire.
▷ ▽ Some of the re-supply which reached the British. In the operation, only ten per cent of the supplies reached the 1st Airborne Division, because the Germans had captured the dropping zones. The paratroopers watched helplessly as the Dakotas braved heavy flak to drop their cargoes to the enemy.
▽ Field-Marshal Walther Model. His aggressive reaction, and the presence of the 9th and 10th Divisions of II S.S. Panzer Corps north of Arnhem, were to unhinge "Market Garden" before it could begin.

1987

△△ *An S.S. officer interrogates two captured soldiers. On the night of September 25/26 the survivors of the Arnhem "Cauldron" had been ordered to withdraw across the Rhine.*
△ *Survivors from the Border Regiment raise a smile for the camera.*
▷ △ *Walking wounded. Over 300 wounded were taken prisoner in the perimeter. Almost ten times that number had already been captured, and were in Dutch hospitals and German dressing stations. Over 1,200 British soldiers were dead, and 3,400 Germans were dead or wounded.*

it was a vast one-way traffic circle, along which raced the life blood of the advancing troops. The driving was hard, the roads merciless on the vehicles, the turnover of equipment staggering, but the supplies were pushed through."

If Operation "Market Garden" proved Allied logistics to have been at fault, it also prejudiced the build-up of a 100-mile salient which was necessary to support Bradley's offensive towards Bonn and Cologne. As Bradley had feared, the British 2nd Army's northwards push ended up between Maastricht, Nijmegen, and Breda. When Antwerp finally got priority Bradley had had to lend two divisions temporarily to 21st Army Group

to help in its capture.

Meanwhile the Canadian 1st Army had seized Le Havre (September 12), Boulogne (September 22), and Calais (October 1), capturing more than 28,000 prisoners. The combined effects of Allied bombardment and German destruction meant that it took longer than expected to get the ports working again. Le Havre in particular had had nearly 10,000 tons of bombs dropped on it and by late October was down to 15 per cent of its capacity. The day after the capture of Boulogne, however, the Allies were able to lay between this port and Dungeness a second 16-tube pipeline, which greatly alleviated the Allied petrol problem.

BRITAIN'S COMMANDOS

Britain's Commandos were born as an act of military defiance in the grim months after Dunkirk.

Churchill had first envisaged them as storm troops to spearhead counter-attacks against the expected German invasion in 1940. But Lieutenant-Colonel Dudley Clark, Military Assistant to the C.I.G.S., suggested that they could be used offensively.

By June 1940, 12 army commandos had been formed. Initially they consisted of ten troops of 50 men, but this was too cumbersome. In October 1940 pairs of commandos were grouped into Special Service Battalions.

Early in 1941 there was a final reorganisation: each commando was to consist of five troops of three officers and 62 men, with a heavy weapons troop of about 40.

The War Office had sent out a circular to commands in the U.K. asking for volunteers for special service of an undefined and hazardous nature. They had to be fully trained soldiers, physically fit, able to swim, and quite incapable of being sea-sick. "Courage, physical endurance, initiative and resource, activity, marksmanship, self-reliance, and an aggressive spirit towards the war" were demanded.

The men came from a wide cross section of the army. Some were Regulars, others Reservists, and Numbers 1 and 2 Commandos had men from the territorial battalions who had operated as independent companies in Norway.

The first Commando raid took place less than three weeks after the force had been conceived. On the night of June 23-24, 120 men landed near Boulogne. There was a brief fire fight and they withdrew.

A raid on Guernsey proved abortive and Churchill growled "Let there be no more silly fiascos like that perpetrated at Guernsey."

Scepticism about the value of the commandos grew in the service ministries. The men themselves began to feel frustrated.

Then on March 4, 1941, Numbers 3 and 4 Commando, with 52 Royal Engineers, conducted the first big raid of the war on the Lofoten Islands off Norway.

It was a complete success; for one casualty the commandos took 216 prisoners, demolished factories and fuel supplies, and captured 11 ships.

Commandos and Combined Operations were now accepted as a lethal and effective weapon.

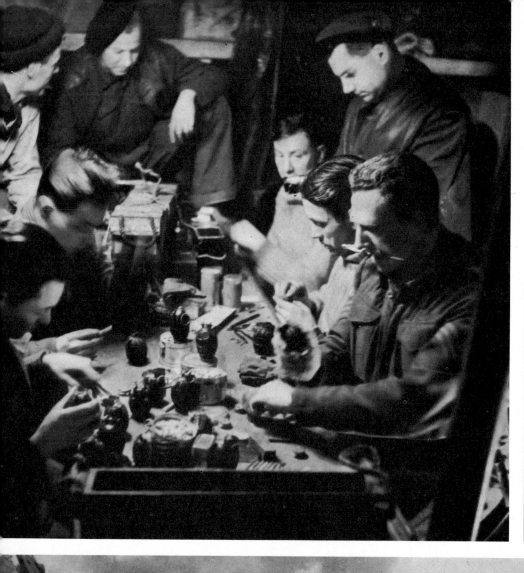

The strategic object of the Vaagsö raid, which was to prompt the Germans to deploy more men in Norway, fulfilled its aim beyond the planners' most optimistic hopes.

The naval forces consisted of a cruiser, four destroyers and two infantry assault ships. The Commandos totalled 590 officers and men.

The raid on December 27, 1941, achieved total surprise. Though the mainland garrison reacted quickly, the battery on Maalöy island was captured in eight minutes.

Fierce street fighting in Vaagsö caused most of the Commando casualties, but the Germans were overwhelmed and the demolition teams completed their work with fire and explosives.

Operation "Archery" yielded 98 prisoners. The raiders lost 20 killed and 57 wounded.

In Hitler's mind "Archery" conjured up images of Norway as a future target for an Allied landing in strength. "Norway is a zone of destiny in this war," he said, and sent reinforcements for the army and navy. By June 1944 the garrison stood at 372,000 men, and they had a very quiet war.

△ ◁ ◁ *Priming hand grenades on the voyage to Vaagsö and Maalöy. The sergeant on the right has his Fairburn knife held in his teeth.*

△ ◁ *Vaagsö seen from Maalöy. In the fighting wooden buildings were burned down to flush out some of the more determined German soldiers.*

△ *Two Commandos assist a wounded comrade to a landing craft. The British lost 20 killed and 57 wounded, while the German losses were never fully confirmed. There were 98 prisoners taken, plus four field guns (Belgian 75-mm guns), an anti-aircraft gun, and a tank destroyed. The Royal Navy disposed of 16,000 tons of shipping.*

◁ ◁ *Soldiers watch as the herring oil factory at Mortenes collapses blazing into Ulversundfjord. Every installation of value to the enemy was destroyed, including the lighthouse and the canning factory on south Vaagsö.*

◁ *Sailors pose with a captured Nazi battle ensign.*

Previous page: *Over the top, 1941-style: the assault party on Maalöy, caught in the glare of a phosphorus bomb.*

1992

The Bruneval raid

The Combined Operations raid on the German radio location station at Bruneval, near Le Havre, was a tactical and moral success. The operation on the night of February 27-28, 1942, boosted the morale of the nation and that of the recently formed 2nd Battalion of the 1st Parachute Brigade. A government paperback on Combined Operations gleefully described the paratroops' brilliant and heroic exploit as "an experiment in radio-dislocation".

A company of paratroops commanded by Major J. D. Frost, with engineers and an R.A.F. radar expert, were to land by parachute near the radar set on the French coast. Their mission was to dismantle as much of it as possible and capture some of its crew. They would then make their way to the beach where the Royal Navy would pick them up.

When Major Frost landed he recognised the country-side from the photographs and briefing model. Collecting his men he led them to the rendezvous point near the isolated house by the radar set.

As his group burst into the house and killed its only occupant, Lieutenant Curtis led his men to the radar set on the cliff. They killed five of the six Germans who were in the adjoining bunkers, and retrieved the sixth, who had fallen over the edge of the cliff and landed on a ledge ten feet below.

With the sound of gunfire coming from the farm house where the local garrison was billeted, Major Frost formed a defensive perimeter round the radar set.

Flight-Sergeant Cox of the R.A.F. and Lieutenant Vernon with his Royal Engineers worked quickly to dismantle the equipment. But now the Germans were closing in, and the group was under fire. Ignoring the danger they worked by torchlight, and though two bullets struck and

damaged some equipment as Flight-Sergeant Cox was holding it, the men completed their task.

Headlights were seen moving toward the German-held farm house, and it was time to go.

As the paratroops started the descent to the beach, they came under fire. There was a stiff fight to secure the beach, because the men who had been detailed for the job had been dropped well away from the correct area because of *Flak*.

On the beach there was an agonising 20 minute wait while the naval force evaded two German destroyers and two E-boats, but at 0235 hours the boats arrived. In the cross-fire from the naval craft and enemy positions, the raiders embarked. The operation had cost the British one killed, seven wounded, and seven missing. The Germans had six killed, an unknown number of wounded, and a gap torn through their radar defences.

△ *The raiders return. Losses from the Bruneval operation were one killed, seven wounded, and seven missing. Spitfires gave air cover to the force at first light, when it was only 15 miles from the French coast.*

△ ◁ *"The Raid on Bruneval" by Richard Eurich, R.A. The paratroops can be seen landing while the embarkation party waits at the foot of the cliff. The withdrawal was not as peaceful as the painting suggests: there was a stiff fire fight to secure the beach, and the naval officer in charge of the landing craft had to use a megaphone to make himself heard over the noise.*

◁ *A scale model of the isolated house and its radar equipment, based on the reconnaissance photograph shown in the insert. On the cliff's edge there is a machine gun post.*

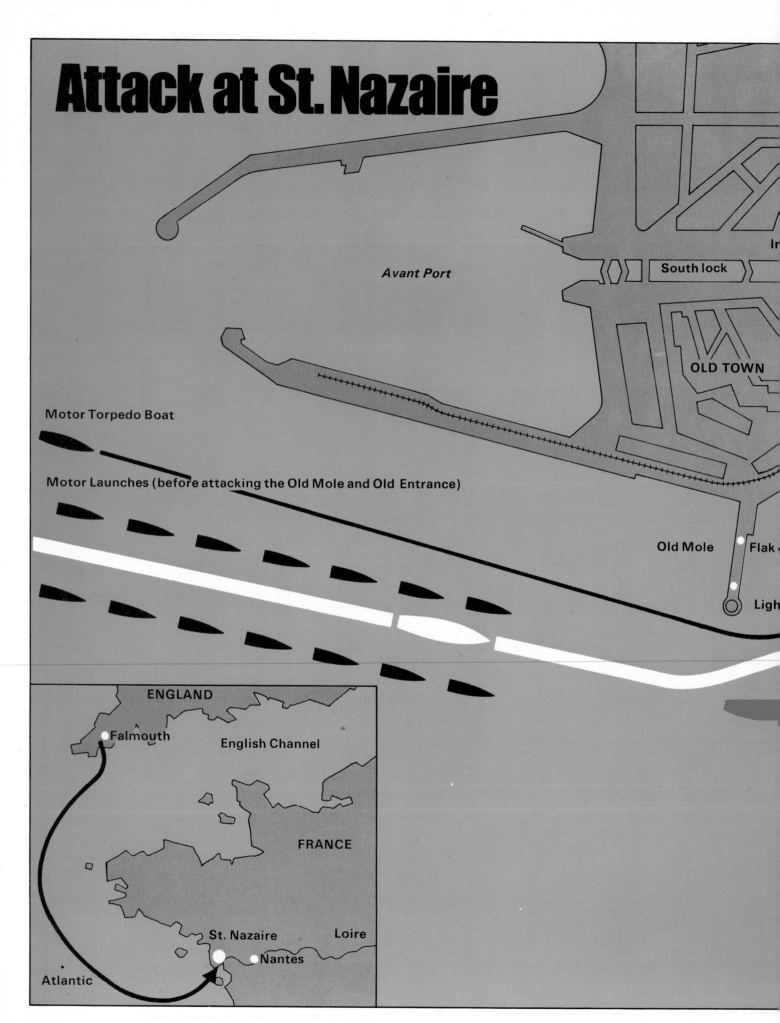

Attack at St.Nazaire

Avant Port

South lock

Ir

OLD TOWN

Motor Torpedo Boat

Motor Launches (before attacking the Old Mole and Old Entrance)

Old Mole

Flak

Ligh

ENGLAND

Falmouth

English Channel

FRANCE

St. Nazaire

Loire

Nantes

Atlantic

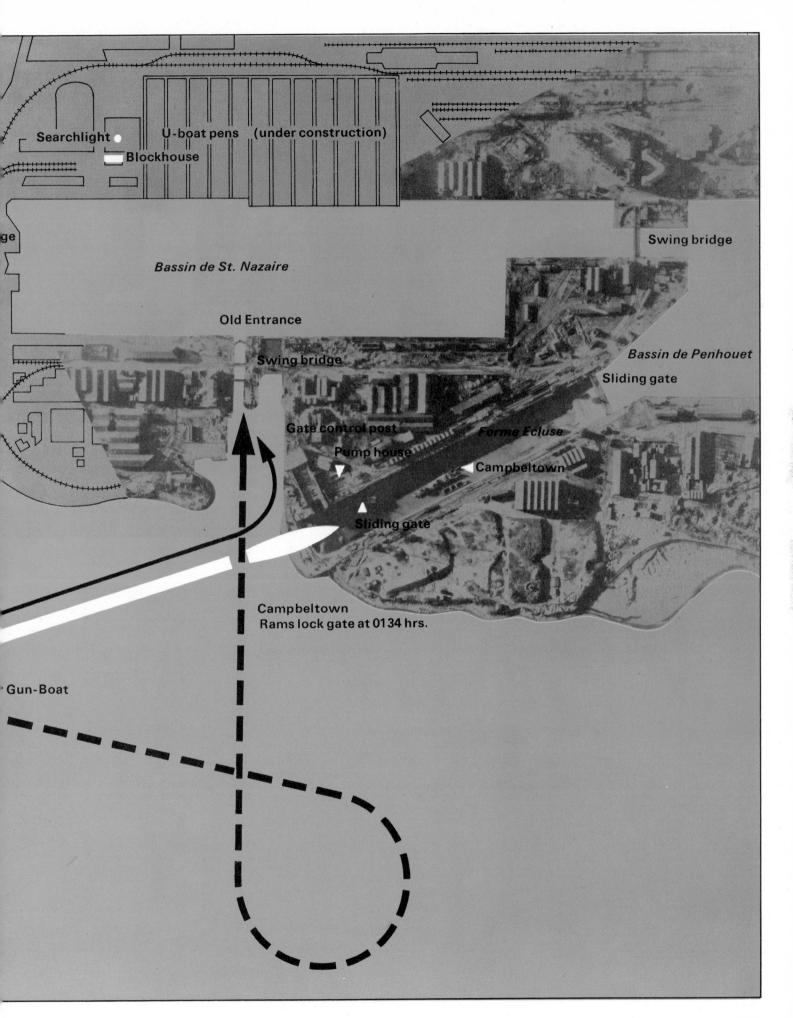

Searchlight

Blockhouse

U-boat pens   (under construction)

Swing bridge

Bassin de St. Nazaire

Old Entrance

Bassin de Penhouet

Swing bridge

Sliding gate

Gate control post

Forme Ecluse

Pump house

Campbeltown

Sliding gate

Campbeltown
Rams lock gate at 0134 hrs.

Gun-Boat

1995

St. Nazaire: the aftermath

▷ *Soldiers and naval personnel are escorted away from the docks.*
▷▷ *A sergeant gives a smart "eyes right" as he leads a file of soldiers past the grave of one of the raiders. The Germans were amazed at the ferocity of the raid, but treated their prisoners generously. At a special parade organised at Lieutenant-Commander Beattie's P.O.W. camp, the German commandant read out the citation for Beattie's V.C.*

▽ Campbeltown, *wedged tight in the lock gates of the* Forme Ecluse. *Her funnels had been cut down to resemble a torpedo boat of the* Möwe *class. German officers can be seen on the bows, where five tons of explosive were soon to go up.*
▽▷ *A German soldier glances at a dead British sergeant as a patrol moves through the docks.*
▽▷▷ *The end of the round-up: a German sailor brings in two soldiers. The Germans remained nervous long after the raid, and Organisation Todt workers in their brown uniforms were shot down when they were mistaken for the khaki of British raiders.*

Operation "Chariot", the raid on the docks at St. Nazaire in March 1942, had as its chief target the destruction of the *Forme Ecluse.*

This was the only Atlantic dry dock big enough to take the German battleship *Tirpitz.* If it was neutralised it could reduce the chances of that ship venturing from her moorings in Norway to attack shipping in the Atlantic.

Commandos in Britain furnished 80 men as demolition experts, while No. 2 Commàndo served as a covering force with about 100 men. The naval force consisted of a destroyer, the *Campbeltown* (loaded with five tons of explosives she would ram the lock gates) and light surface craft to transport the Commandos. The date was fixed for March 28.

The last stage of the journey up the Loire was made under German colours. Signals were sent to the shore batteries in German saying that the ships had been damaged and requesting permission to proceed to St. Nazaire.

In five tense minutes they passed the main batteries without receiving any damage. At 0127 hours the Germans opened fire in earnest, the *Campbeltown* hauled down the false colours, hoisted the White Ensign and returned the fire.

At 0134 she crashed into the lock gates. The main part of the operation was complete.

Then the Commandos went into action. They attacked the two control posts for the dry dock gates, and demolished the pump house and a bridge at the northern end of the docks. Two tugs were attacked with charges below the water line.

Throughout these operations the naval force had been exchanging heavy fire at close range with the ships in the port and shore emplacements.

Of the 18 craft which had entered the Loire estuary, only two launches returned safely to England. Only five men managed to return home overland, while 169 of their comrades were killed. The rest were sent into prison camps.

Some time after 1000 hours the charges on the *Campbeltown* exploded, demolishing the lock gate.

The *Tirpitz* never ventured from her Norwegian lair, for the *Forme Ecluse* was out of action for the rest of the war.

1997

Skorzeny: Hitler's ace com

The discreet arrest of Mussolini, following his interview with King Victor Emmanuel on July 25, 1943, left the Germans with a double problem: find the former Duce, and having found him, rescue him.

The task fell to Otto Skorzeny, a *Waffen*-S.S. officer running a commando training school at Friedenthal, near Berlin.

When he began his search, Italy was still an ally of Germany. But if the Italians could hold Mussolini until their surrender to the Allies, he could be a trump card in the negotiations.

Skorzeny traced Mussolini to an island prison near Sardinia. He laid careful plans, took aerial photographs, and was about to launch the operation when a final check showed that the Duce had gone. It was a lucky discovery, for Hitler had warned him that failure would mean dismissal and a public repudiation.

Back in Rome Skorzeny intercepted a code message to the Italian Ministry of Interior; it read: "SECURITY MEASURES AROUND GRAN SASSO COMPLETED. CUELI" Skorzeny had discovered that General Cueli was the official responsible for the Duce's safety.

The only place in Gran Sasso, a mountainous part of the Apennines, which could house a state prisoner with his guards, was the winter sports hotel of Campo Imperatore. Built on a 6,000-foot crag, it could only be reached by a funicular railway.

On September 8, Italy surrendered. The operation was now military rather than diplomatic.

Skorzeny established that there was at least a battalion of *Carabinieri* in the area and a further 250 men in the hotel. His reconnaisance photographs showed a triangular patch of land near the hotel. Paratroops could not land there (the air was too thin), but gliders might.

The Luftwaffe eventually agreed to provide gliders for the 90 Luftwaffe troops and the 20 men from Skorzeny's unit.

On the afternoon of September 12 they set off.

The landing zone proved to be a sloping, rock-studded, shelf. But risking destruction Skorzeny shouted to his pilot, "Dive—crash land! As near the hotel as you can."

With a shuddering, bouncing skid and a rending crash the glider came to a halt.

The soldiers leapt out and raced the 20 yards across to the hotel.

Skorzeny recognised a familiar shaved head at an upper window. "Get back!" he yelled at Mussolini, "Get back from the window."

By sheer surprise and aggressiveness they over-whelmed the guards without firing a shot.

The *Carabinieri* crowded in the corridors were too close to shoot, and the Germans barged past them and pushed further into the hotel.

Skorzeny burst into a room, and there, with two Italian officers, was the Duce. As the Germans came through the door, two more climbed up the lightning conductor and through the window.

Skorzeny now summoned the Italian colonel who had been the Duce's gaoler.

"I ask your immediate surrender. Mussolini is already in our hands. We hold the building. If you want to avert senseless bloodshed you have 60 seconds to go and reflect."

The bluff worked and the colonel returned with a goblet of wine, for "a gallant victor".

The return trip was no less

mando

hazardous. Captain Gerlach landed a Fieseler *Storch* on a strip cleared on the narrow landing zone.

Then loaded with the substantial bulk of Skorzeny and Mussolini the *Storch* took off. It was held by 12 men as its engine revved to a high pitch, but even then the take-off was only achieved after the *Storch* lurched across the mountain side and plunged headlong over the edge of a ravine.

They landed at Rome and transferred to a transport plane. Skorzeny had completed his mission – overnight he had changed from an obscure S.S. officer to a national hero.

Dr. Goebbels, the Reich Propaganda Minister, noted in his diary: "Even upon the enemy the effect of this melodramatic deliverance is enormous . . . We are able to celebrate a first-class moral victory."

▷ *Otto Skorzeny, photographed on his surrender in 1945. His rescue of Mussolini from the Gran Sasso and use of German troops dressed as Americans during the "Battle of the Bulge" gave him considerable notoriety with the Allies.*
▽ ◁ *Paratroopers race across the rocky plateau, which was later to serve as a hazardous landing strip for the Fieseler* Storch *which would fly Mussolini to "freedom".*
▽ *Skorzeny, on the extreme left, with Mussolini. With words deemed suitable for the dramatic rescue he had greeted the latter: "Duce, I have been sent by the Führer to set you free." Mussolini replied: "I knew my friend Adolf Hitler would not abandon me. I embrace my liberator."*

◁ A shabby 60-year old Italian struggles into a German spotter plane. It is hard to recognise Italy's Duce in the last months of his life.

▷ With Mussolini in the cramped cockpit, Skorzeny squeezes in, his 6 feet 4 inches frame further congesting the overcrowded space. Twelve men hung on to the Storch while it ran its engine up fully, and then when they let go it raced across the scree, buckled its port wheel, and only became airborne when it had plunged over a ravine.

▽ Kaltenbrunner watches, at the left, as Hitler greets Skorzeny at the Wolfsschanze. Earlier on the telephone Hitler had said: "Skorzeny, you are a man after my own heart. You have gained the day and crowned our mission with success. Your Führer thanks you!"

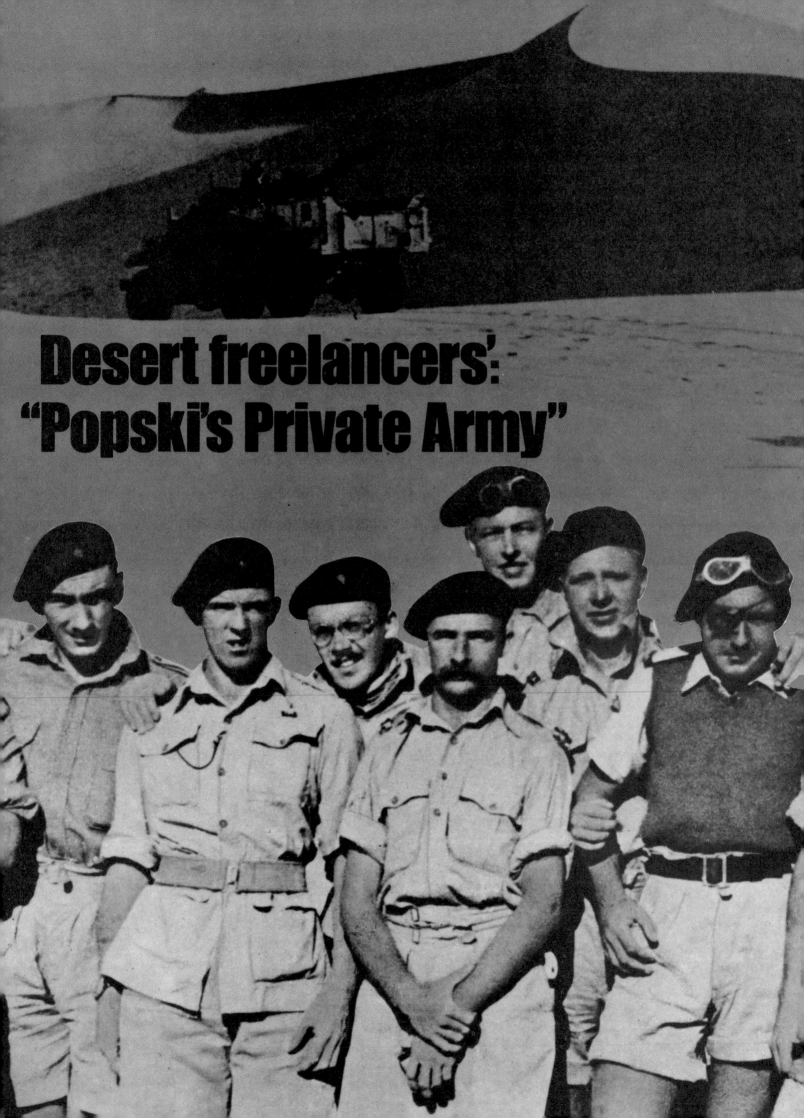

Desert freelancers': "Popski's Private Army"

Vladimir Peniakoff, born 1897 in Belgium, became a sugar manufacturer in Egypt in the inter-war years. Here he developed desert navigation skills which he would employ leading a raiding force known as "Popski's Private Army". Popski was a great admirer of the British way of life and had been an undergraduate at Cambridge before joining the French Army in World War I. In World War II he joined the British Army and wanted to become a member of the Long Range Desert Group, but he was persuaded to form his own group, which was first known as No. 1 Long Range Demolition Squadron, though it soon earned the official title Popski's Private Army. It carried its own style of reconnaissance and demolition in North Africa and Italy, attacking petrol dumps and other installations.

1. *The astrolabe badge of Popski's Private Army. The early badges were made of brass, but some white metal and silver versions were made later in Italy.*
2. *Vladimir Peniakoff, Belgian adventurer of Russian origin, who led his raiding force in Africa and Italy.*
3. *Popski's jeep.*
4. *Popski, with a hook for a left hand, and Cpl. Cokes, with 50 skin grafts on his legs, near the end of the war.*

The American/British L.R.D.G. Chevrolet 30-cwt 4 x 2 truck

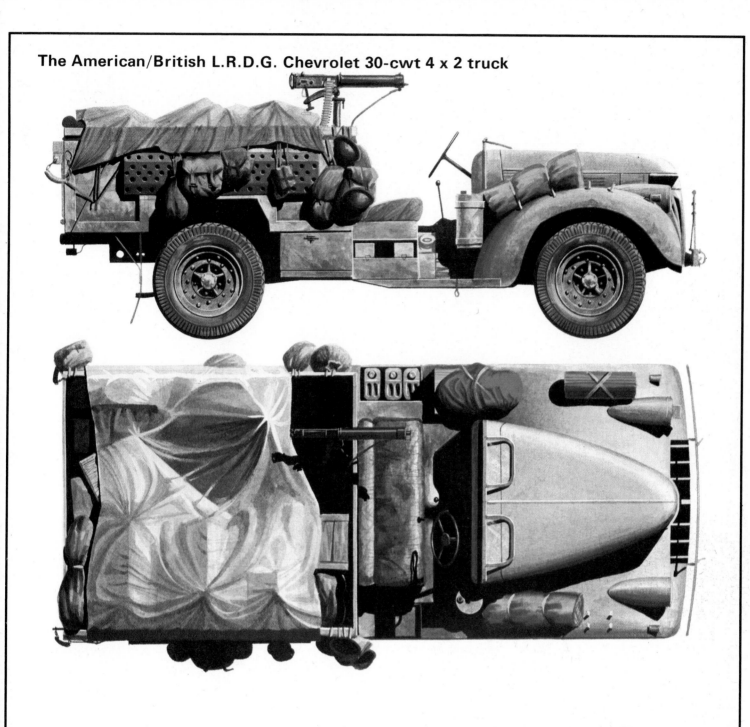

Wheelbase: 134 inches.
Engine: one Chevrolet 6-cylinder inline, 85-hp.
Range: over 1,000 miles.
Capacity: 2 tons of stores.
Armament: one .303-inch Vickers machine gun and the crew's personal weapons.

2005

2006

"No. 1 Demolition Squadron", better known as "Popski's Private Army" was one of several reconnaissance and raiding units spawned by the 8th Army in Africa.

Vladimir Peniakoff (his name was changed by British signallers to Popski) was a Belgian of Russian origin. He had settled in Cairo before the war and developed a taste for desert travel.

He volunteered for service in the British Army, and in 1942 formed a commando of 23 Arabs with a British sergeant.

With this force he collected Intelligence, attacked an Italian petrol dump, and arranged escape routes for prisoners-of-war.

At the end of 1942 he served in an L.R.D.G. patrol and lost a finger in a raid on the strategically important Barce airfield.

He wanted to remain with the L.R.D.G., who had taught him desert skills and shown him equipment like the sun compass, condenser, and sand channels, but was persuaded by Colonel Hackett of the Middle East Headquarters to form his own special long-range unit.

The name was Hackett's invention: he suggested it as a joke, but the title Popski's Private Army was accepted by the Middle East H.Q.

Popski set out with 23 men in four armed jeeps and two three-ton trucks. This first venture was unsuccessful for most of the vehicles were captured or destroyed by the Germans.

Drawing new jeeps from the 8th Army, he moved into southern Tunisia. In operations south of the Mareth Line his jeeps were destroyed by fighters, and his unit marched 115 miles in the desert before being picked up by friendly forces.

Popski conducted some further limited operations in Africa before the Axis surrender in May 1943.

P.P.A. landed at Taranto soon after the Italian armistice in 1943. Its mission was to ascertain German strength in southern Italy.

This was accomplished through the public telephone system: Italian officers, now new allies, rang their colleagues, who gave a situation report on German moves in their area, telephone communications still being intact after the invasion and armistice.

Popski's major coup came when, dressed in British khaki drill, he passed himself off as an Italian and called at the German headquarters in Gravina. Here he stole a list of all the men on the

ration strength of the 1st Parachute Division, a premier German formation operating in southern Italy.

P.P.A. expanded and began to operate in separate patrols. They consisted of five or six jeeps each mounting a .3-inch and a .5-inch machine gun. The latter fired in succession tracer, armour-piercing, and incendiary rounds. With stowed fuel the jeeps had a range of 600 miles. The patrols carried mines and explosives and their own water and rations.

Near Salerno Italian peasants brought him Brigadier Klopper, who had been captured at Tobruk with the 2nd South African Division. He had escaped in Italy after the armistice.

Besides enlarging their conventional forces (they numbered 118 by the end of the war) P.P.A. collected two Russian P.O.W.'s, Ivan and Nikolai.

Popski's Private Army co-operated with Italian partisans, harried small German garrisons and the lines of communication, and reconnoitred routes for the Allied armies.

In a local counter-attack in 1944 in northern Italy Popski lost his left hand.

After a spell in hospital, Popski led patrols which made contact with Russians in Austria in 1945.

△ ◁ *Jeeps of Popski's Private Army move cautiously along a country lane in the Apennines.*
◁ *P.P.A. jeeps pull off the road into a defensive position. The vehicle in the foreground is armed with a .5-inch Browning M2 heavy machine gun and a .3-inch Browning M1919A4 machine gun. All the P.P.A. vehicles carried a heavy fire power, some being armed with two M2's. Popski's Private Army was about 200 strong, and though it had the reputation of being a dare-devil unit, Popski asserted that all his operations were based on careful planning and he took few risks.*
△ *P.P.A. jeeps laager up in the Apennines. The men have pitched their bivouac tents by their jeeps and found time for some washing.*

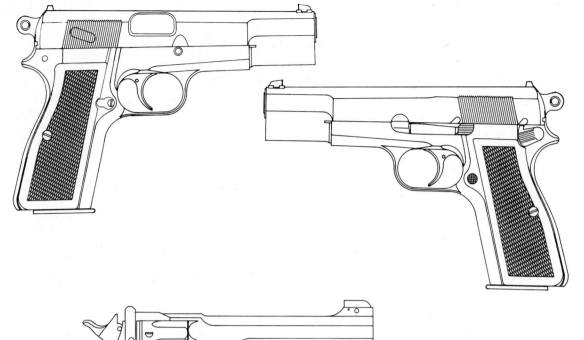

The Canadian Inglis 9-mm Pistol, Browning, Hi-Power, No. 2 Mark 1

Calibre: *9-mm Parabellum.*
Operation: *recoil, semi-automatic.*
Weight: *1.9 lbs.*
Overall length: *8 inches.*
Barrel length: *4.75 inches.*
Feed: *detachable double-row box magazine with 13 rounds.*
Front sight: *blade.*
Rear sight: *vee notch.*
Muzzle velocity: *1040 to 1500 feet per second depending on ammunition.*

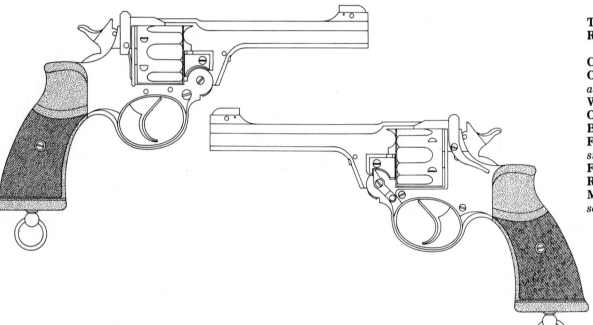

The British Enfield .38-inch Revolver No. 2 Mark 1

Calibre: *.38-inch.*
Operation: *single or double action.*
Weight: *1.58 lbs.*
Overall length: *10.25 inches.*
Barrel length: *5 inches.*
Feed: *revolving cylinder with six chambers.*
Front sight: *blade.*
Rear sight: *square notch.*
Muzzle velocity: *600 feet per second.*

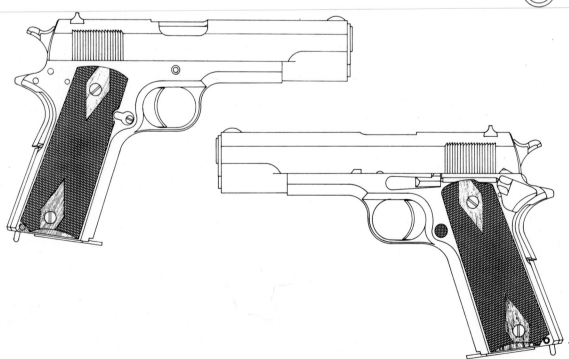

The American Colt Calibre .45-inch Model 1911 Automatic Pistol

Calibre: *.45-inch.*
Operation: *recoil, semi-automatic.*
Weight: *2.43 lbs.*
Overall length: *8.62 inches.*
Barrel length: *5 inches.*
Feed: *detachable inline box magazine with seven rounds.*
Front sight: *blade.*
Rear sight: *square notch.*
Muzzle velocity: *830 feet per second.*

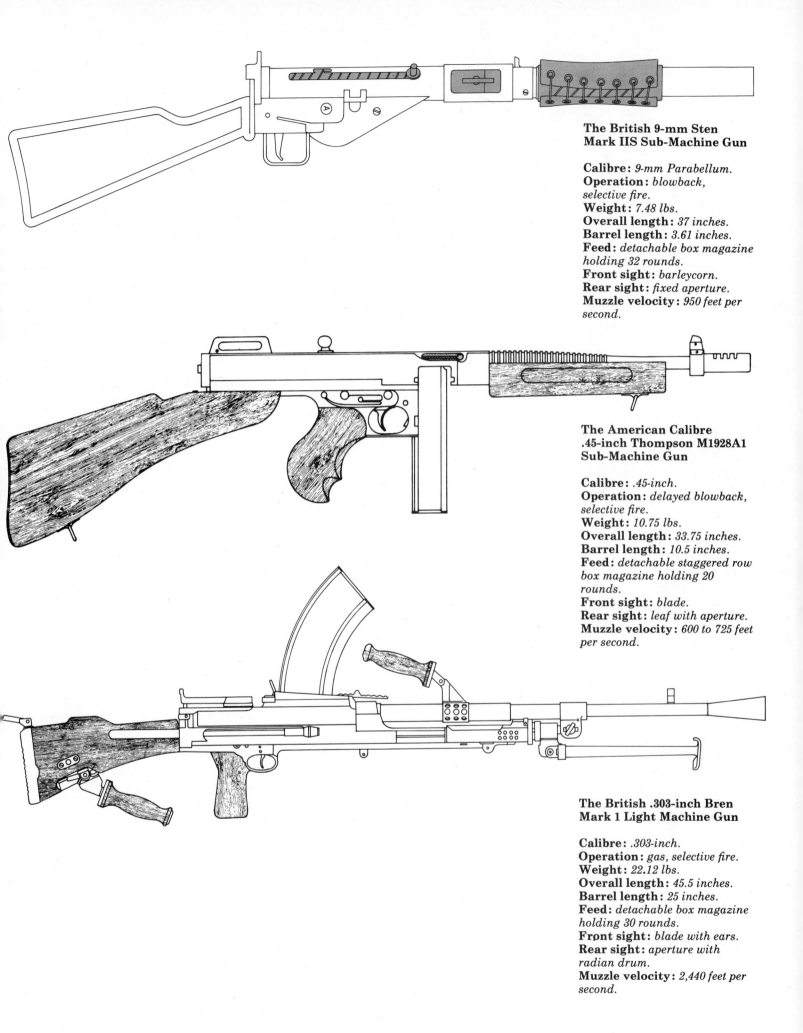

The British 9-mm Sten Mark IIS Sub-Machine Gun

Calibre: *9-mm Parabellum.*
Operation: *blowback, selective fire.*
Weight: *7.48 lbs.*
Overall length: *37 inches.*
Barrel length: *3.61 inches.*
Feed: *detachable box magazine holding 32 rounds.*
Front sight: *barleycorn.*
Rear sight: *fixed aperture.*
Muzzle velocity: *950 feet per second.*

The American Calibre .45-inch Thompson M1928A1 Sub-Machine Gun

Calibre: *.45-inch.*
Operation: *delayed blowback, selective fire.*
Weight: *10.75 lbs.*
Overall length: *33.75 inches.*
Barrel length: *10.5 inches.*
Feed: *detachable staggered row box magazine holding 20 rounds.*
Front sight: *blade.*
Rear sight: *leaf with aperture.*
Muzzle velocity: *600 to 725 feet per second.*

The British .303-inch Bren Mark 1 Light Machine Gun

Calibre: *.303-inch.*
Operation: *gas, selective fire.*
Weight: *22.12 lbs.*
Overall length: *45.5 inches.*
Barrel length: *25 inches.*
Feed: *detachable box magazine holding 30 rounds.*
Front sight: *blade with ears.*
Rear sight: *aperture with radian drum.*
Muzzle velocity: *2,440 feet per second.*

The first Commandos were formed in June 1940, each consisting of ten troops of 50 men. Later, in 1941, they were reorganised into five troops of 65, with a heavy weapons platoon of 40. The original name suggested by the War Office was Special Service Battalions, but the initials "S.S." smacked too much of the Nazi Schutzstaffel so the units were later named after the Boer troops commanded by such men as General Smuts. The Commandos were drawn from men of all the Allied nations fighting with the British. They attended a gruelling 12 week course at the depot at Achnacarry Castle 14 miles from Fort William. The titles (the shoulder badge with the corps or regiment's name) and the flashes (the badge with the unit insignia) and the cap badges of the British Army and Marine Commando units are shown in this montage.

1. The Salamander flash of Number 1 Commando. 2. The Fairburn knife of No. 2 Commando, which featured both as a flash and a cap badge. 3. The Combined Operations sign, which depicts the three fighting arms in one flash. 4. The crossed daggers of 5 Commando. 5. The Dolphin flash of 101 Troop 6 Commando. 6. The skull insignia of the depot unit. 7. A representation of the black hackle of 9 Commando. 8. 5 Troop flash. 9. H.Q. Special Service Brigade. 10. Knuckle-duster knife cap badge of the Middle East Commandos. 11. Special Boat Service. 12. Parachute wings worn by parachute troop of 12 Commando. 13. Cap badge of Free French Commandos attached to 4 Commando. 14. The Commando flash. 15. Cap badge of the Royal Marines worn by Marine Commandos.

SAS: the winged sword

▽ *Lieutenant-Colonel David Stirling with some of his desert raiders. Rommel paid tribute to Stirling and the S.A.S. in his diary. "These Commandos, working from Kufra and the Qattara Depression, sometimes operated right up into Cyrenaica, where they caused considerable havoc and seriously disquieted the Italians". He described Stirling as the "very able and adaptable commander of the desert group which had caused us more damage than any other unit of equal strength".*

▷ *A resupply drop in France in 1944. In 1944 there were British, French, and Belgian S.A.S. contingents operating in northern Europe. Radio communications with Britain presented a problem for raiders who had to carry the minimum of equipment.*

The Special Air Service was conceived by a young Commando officer as he was recovering from a training accident in North Africa in 1941.

Lieutenant David Stirling felt that the commando principle of large forces being launched on a single raid was wasteful. A third of the force had to be used to hold the beach-head while the remainder conducted the assault and demolitions.

His scheme would employ about six men, who would place charges with delay fuses on targets like aircraft. By the time the charges exploded the raiders would be far away. Sixty men with 12 charges each could destroy the Axis air force on the ground in simultaneous raids.

In an audacious "raid" in July 1941, Stirling visited the Middle East Headquarters. He had no permit to enter the building, and had to worm his way through a small gap in the barbed-wire fence. Risking arrest he tried doors in the building and found General Ritchie, Deputy Chief-of-Staff, Middle East Forces. His idea was forwarded to General Auchinleck, who gave it his approval. It was economical; six officers and 60 men were not a vast loss to the 8th Army, and if they succeeded the effects of the raid could be dramatic.

The name of the force, "L Detachment of the Special Air Service Brigade" was a staff office invention to deceive the enemy into the belief that there were paratroops in North Africa.

The first operation, on November 17, 1941, was a parachute attack on five forward fighter and bomber airfields at Tmimi and Gazala. Unfortunately heavy sand storms caused the force to be dropped in the wrong area and

the operation was a complete failure, only 22 of the original 63 men surviving.

The S.A.S. launched no more parachute attacks in the Middle East. Instead they used the Long Range Desert Group for transport and between December 1941 and March 1942 made about 20 raids behind the enemy lines, destroying 115 aircraft and numerous vehicles.

Having proved its worth, "L Detachment" was expanded. Rommel was later to pay it the compliment that it "caused us more damage than any other unit of equal strength".

The S.A.S. insignia was adopted about this time. A winged sword, it symbolised King Arthur's sword Excalibur, the weapon which would win freedom from the invader. Its colours, dark and light blue, were chosen because the original unit had had a number from both the Oxford

2013

R. B. "Paddy" Mayne, a pre-war Irish rugby football international, succeeded Stirling as the commanding officer of the S.A.S. By the end of the war Mayne had destroyed more aircraft than any man alive and had been awarded the D.S.O. and three bars, becoming the most decorated soldier in the British Army. An enthusiast for action, he was unhappy when he was ordered to run recruit training at the S.A.S. base at Kabrit, where he proved a poor administrator.

David Stirling was born in 1915 and joined the Commandos in 1940, serving with "Layforce" in the Middle East. In July he presented plans to Generals Ritchie and Auchinleck for a special force to attack enemy airfields. In December, operating from Jalo, they destroyed 90 aircraft in two weeks and Stirling was given permission to expand the unit. To the Germans he was known as the "Phantom Major". On January 10, 1943 he was captured by German soldiers who had been brought in to track down the S.A.S. As a persistent escaper he was sent to Colditz Castle.

◁ An S.A.S. jeep in desert guise. It is fitted with twin Vickers K machine guns, a condenser on the radiator grill, and carries fuel in a collection of American and German petrol cans. The crew wear caps bearing the S.A.S. badge, the winged sword with the motto "Who Dares Wins".

▷ S.A.S. jeep in the European theatre. At the wheel is Major Ian Fenwick, who led a group from 1st S.A.S. in Operation "Gain". Ten men were killed, including Major Fenwick, in the operation, which cut rail communications between Rambouillet, Provins, Gien, Orléans, and Chartres.

▽ A Vickers machine gun crew in northern Italy. The man on the left carries the 50-lb tripod, the one in the centre the 33-lb gun, and the man on the right the 7½ pints of water to cool the barrel. Over long ranges the curving trajectory of the weapon could be used for a plunging fire effect.

△ *Men of the French S.A.S. battalions marching down the Champs Elysées in 1944. They operated in the Brittany area and the Vosges during the summer of 1944, attacking German convoys, mining roads and supporting* Maquis *groups. The units in the Brittany area suffered heavy casualties in a vigorous German counter-attack, but though lightly armed they were better soldiers with local support and knowledge, and so for the loss of 32 men they killed 155 of the enemy. In fighting near Orléans, French S.A.S. units linked up to attack the German lines of communication, and in late August and early September captured 18,000 Germans. Lacking the facilities to handle such large numbers they presented them to an officer of an advanced American unit – to his considerable surprise. After the liberation of Paris the companies were withdrawn for a rest and refit. They were later employed in Belgium and in the follow-up to Operation "Varsity".*

and Cambridge University boat race crews.

The S.A.S. evolved a style of warfare in the desert which, with some alterations, would typify their operations throughout the war.

The jeep, which was becoming available through Lend-Lease sources, served as their steed. Loaded with ammunition and fuel, and stripped of excess fittings, it was equipped with a variety of automatic weapons. The Vickers K machine gun, formerly fitted in Gloster Gladiator fighters, was adapted to a ground rôle. Mounted in pairs, with a rate of fire of 1,200 rounds a minute, they were effective against men, soft-skinned vehicles, and parked aircraft. Later the jeeps were fitted with .5-inch Brownings, in addition to the personal weapons of the crew. In France and Italy they supplemented this with a variety of mortars and anti-tank weapons, and even sometimes a 75-mm pack howitzer.

By April 1942 the S.A.S. had expanded to include French and Greek soldiers, and at the beginning of 1943 the establishment stood at about 1,100 officers and men. Of these a high proportion were officers and N.C.O.s. Though the S.A.S. has been criticised

for the large numbers of first-class men it absorbed, it is arguable that they did more damage to the enemy in this force than they could if they had been in a conventional unit.

As the war in North Africa drew to a close the nature of S.A.S. operations changed. The 1st S.A.S. Regiment (formed from the original L Detachment) was split into the Special Raiding Squadron and a Special Boat Squadron. In May 1943 it was joined by the 2nd S.A.S. Regiment, and together they raided Crete, Sardinia, and the Greek islands, and took part in the invasion of Sicily and Italy.

At the end of 1943 the regiments returned to Britain in preparation for the invasion of Europe. They now consisted of the 1st and 2nd Regiments and 3rd and 4th French Parachute Battalions and a Belgian Independent Parachute Squadron.

From June 6 to October 31, 1944, the S.A.S. Brigade carried out 43 operations, delivered and supplied by Nos. 38 and 46 Groups of the R.A.F.

Using Brittany as a base they attacked the communications to the Normandy bridgehead. When the Allies broke out, the S.A.S. turned to harrying the retreating enemy. Losses were heavy in

these operations, however.

In secret directives, Hitler paid the S.A.S. and Commandos a dubious compliment – German commanders were to "slaughter to the last man all those who take part in Commando engagements" and S.A.S. troops "must be handed over at once to the nearest Gestapo unit. These men are very dangerous and the presence of S.A.S. troops in any area must be immediately reported. They must be ruthlessly exterminated."

S.A.S. forces expanded after the landings in Normandy and took their war to central and southern France, Belgium, and Holland.

Late in 1944 when the fighting had been stabilised along the Rhine, the 3rd Squadron, 2nd S.A.S. Regiment, was sent to Italy to co-operate with Italian partisans.

With the break-out over the Rhine, the S.A.S. spearheaded the final offensive, capturing key bridges and airfields in Holland and Germany. In Norway, 1 and 2 S.A.S. had a share in the surrender of the German garrison held by 300,000 men.

At the end of the war the French and Belgian regiments became part of their respective armies, while the British regiments were disbanded.

CHAPTER 133

Finland drops out

The dramatic circumstances in which Field-Marshal Model just managed to hold the Soviet push between the Niemen and the Carpathians have already been noted. On August 16 he was recalled to replace Kluge as C.-in-C. West, and handed over command of Army Group "Centre" to Colonel-General Reinhardt, while Army Group "North Ukraine" passed from his hands into those of Colonel-General Harpe, under the title of Army Group "A".

Until the end of December, Marshal Rokossovsky and General Zakharov, commanders respectively of the 1st and 2nd Belorussian Fronts, restricted themselves to operations with limited objectives. Halfway through September Rokossovsky, with 70 divisions, had taken his revenge for the check he had received six weeks previously on the approach to Warsaw. He had fallen back to Wołomin and reoccupied Praga, on the outskirts of the Polish capital. The German defenders were at the end of their tether. Further north, Rokossovsky had pushed as far as Modlin at the confluence of the Bug and the Vistula.

On his right, Zakharov, at the head of 71 infantry divisions and five tank corps, had penetrated the corridor between the Bug and the Narew. On the right bank of the latter he had taken a wide bridgehead around Pułtusk from the German 2nd Army (Colonel-General Weiss). And so, between the 2nd and 3rd Belorussian Fronts—the latter still under the command of Colonel-General Chernyakhovsky—the outline of the pincer movement which would lead to the encirclement and then the conquest of East Prussia was forming.

Puppet government

Meanwhile, behind the Polish front, a series of events of great importance for the future was taking place. First of all, east of the Curzon Line the Russians established—or purely and simply restored—their own authority. Moreover, a "Polish Committee of National Liberation" was set up in Lublin under the Communist E. B. Osóbka-Morawski,

▽ *Finnish infantry in 1944. Although they had managed to hold the Russians in the terrible winter of 1939-1940, the Finns now had good weather, as well as battle-hardened Russian troops, to struggle against. It was to be an impossible task.*

△ *Russian infantry double over a pontoon bridge across the Bug, under cover of a smoke screen. Despite its enormous numerical superiority, however, the Red Army was still finding considerable difficulty in forcing the Germans back.*

▽ *Radio operators of the Home Army keep the Russians informed of the situation in Poland.*

who was so totally submissive to the Kremlin that he made no protest when the Russians systematically organised a persecution of the Polish Home Army fighters on Polish soil.

The Baltic states overrun

At Tukums, as has been described, the 1st Baltic Front (General Bagramyan) had cut the last land contact between Army Group "North" (Colonel-General Schörner) and the other armies of the Reich. But Bagramyan was himself attacked on August 16 and his flank turned by the 3rd *Panzerarmee,* now under Colonel-General Raus after Reinhardt's promotion. It had been reinforced to the strength of two Panzer corps, with five Panzer divisions and the *"Grossdeutschland" Panzergrenadier* Division. It launched its attack from the region north of Taurage and met few difficulties other than the natural ones of terrain. By August 20, it had covered 125 miles and had established a solid link with the right wing of the 16th Army near Tukums.

Guderian clashes with Hitler

This new Russian success led to a clash between Hitler and the new Chief-of-Staff of O.K.H., Colonel-General Guderian. Guderian tried in vain to impress upon the Führer that he should use this temporary respite to evacuate Estonia and the eastern part of Lithuania as quickly as possible, though maintaining a bridgehead around Riga. In this way, more solidity would be given to Army Group "North", which would then have some chance of success in checking the Russians. The Führer cut him short sharply. To abandon Tallinn and Paldiski, he said, would automatically provoke the "defection" of Finland.

Was he unaware that this was as good as complete already? In any event he

was informed of the Finno-Soviet armistice on September 3, 1944, and this cut away the ground from his argument. Nevertheless, he refused to send new orders to Colonel-General Schörner. This time he lyingly claimed the support of Grand-Admiral Dönitz when he spoke to Guderian. But by now Army Group "North" had only 32 divisions to put into the field against 130 Russian ones of the Leningrad and three Baltic Fronts.

Estonia invaded

Overwhelming *Armeegruppe* "Narva" by September 24, Marshal Govorov's Leningrad Front had occupied Estonia almost completely. Then his 8th Army (General Paern), using American landing-craft, began, first with Moon and Dagö, to take the islands in the Gulf of Riga defended by the 23rd and 218th Divisions. With the aid of a naval force under Vice-Admiral Thiele, including the pocket-battleships *Lützow* and *Scheer* and the cruisers that Hitler had wanted to send to the scrapyard, these two divisions managed to hold out on the Sworbe peninsula against six Soviet divisions until November 23 and then cross over to Kurland without too many losses. This was the first example on the Eastern Front of those amphibious retreats which the Kriegsmarine would effect, saving the Army serious losses of men and equipment.

Riga falls to Eremenko

On October 13, the advance parties of General A. I. Eremenko's 3rd Baltic Front had entered Riga. The day after Colonel-General Raus's success, Guderian had obtained Hitler's approval for a directive requiring Army Group "North" to transfer the 3rd *Panzerarmee* from the south to halt the Russian drive on Memel. But Schörner did nothing about it, for he did not believe that Memel was in danger.

While Guderian vainly pleaded with

▽ *The commander of a Polish armoured unit serving with the Red Army gives his orders. Note the predominantly Russian uniform worn.*

The German Heinkel He 111H-20/R3 bomber

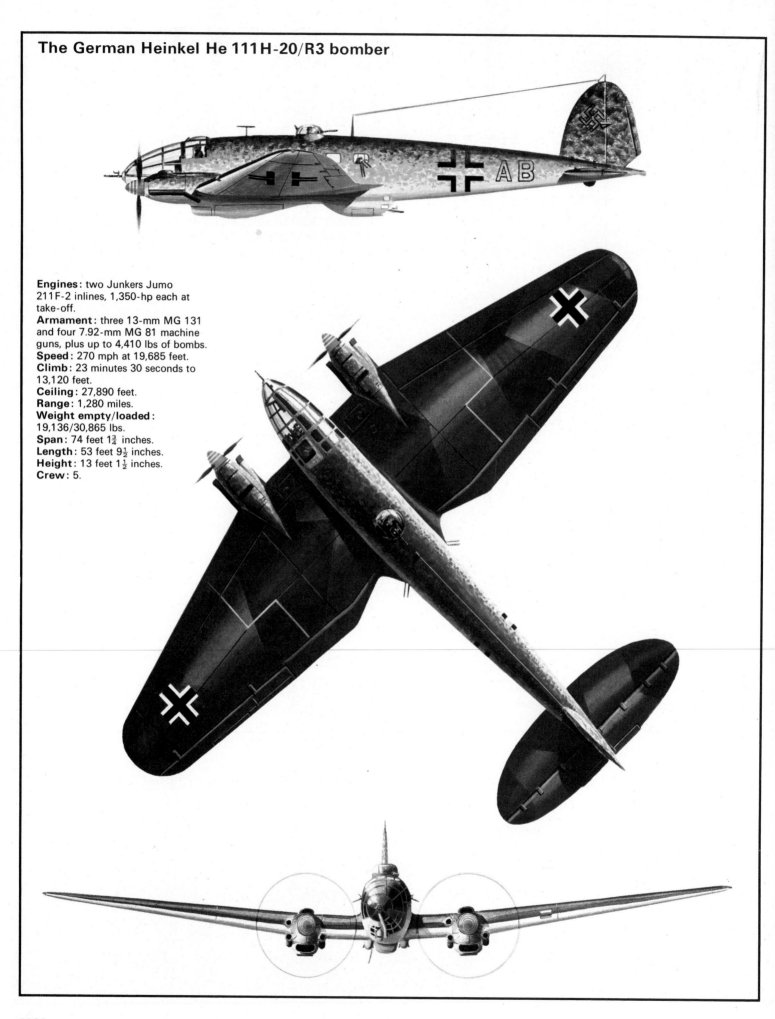

Engines: two Junkers Jumo 211F-2 inlines, 1,350-hp each at take-off.
Armament: three 13-mm MG 131 and four 7.92-mm MG 81 machine guns, plus up to 4,410 lbs of bombs.
Speed: 270 mph at 19,685 feet.
Climb: 23 minutes 30 seconds to 13,120 feet.
Ceiling: 27,890 feet.
Range: 1,280 miles.
Weight empty/loaded: 19,136/30,865 lbs.
Span: 74 feet 1¾ inches.
Length: 53 feet 9½ inches.
Height: 13 feet 1½ inches.
Crew: 5.

Schörner, the *Stavka* had discovered that the road to Memel was very weakly held by the Germans. And so, on September 24, General Bagramyan received the order to transfer the centre of gravity of the 1st Baltic Front without delay from the Mitau area to the Siauliai region, exactly where Guderian wanted to place the 3rd *Panzerarmee,* and to break the German line at that point.

Communications cut

The attack began on October 5. On the first day 14 divisions and four armoured corps (more than 500 tanks) breached Schörner's defensive screen. Covering a distance of 90 miles in five days, Bagramyan reached the Baltic at Palanga, 15 miles north of Memel. For the second time, Army Group "North" which, on October 10, had 26 divisions, including two Panzer, found itself cut off. It is true that it received supplies by sea and that the Kurland pocket, along the Tukums–Auce–Weinoden–south of Liepāja

line, was about half the size of Belgium. In spite of this, once Bagramyan had made his drive, there was no way of maintaining the German 18th Army around Riga.

In contrast, Colonel-General Chernyakhovsky received a bloody check on his first attempt to invade East Prussia. And yet the 3rd Belorussian Front put about 40 divisions into the line, strongly backed by armour and aircraft, over a front of 90 miles, while the German 4th Army could muster only 15 on a front of 220 miles between the Niemen and the Narew at Nowogród.

But the defence was commanded by a resolute leader, General F. Hossbach, and had the advantages of permanent fortifications. Moreover, the Soviet attack did not enjoy the benefit of surprise. At the beginning (October 16-19) the 11th Guards Army, which formed Chernyakhovsky's spearhead,

managed to break General Matzky's XXVI Corps and advance 30 miles over the same east-west line that had been followed by the Russian forces under General Rennenkampf in August 1914. Meanwhile, further to the south, the 31st Army took Gołdap.

Withdrawing five or six divisions from his less threatened sectors, Hossbach managed to seal the breaches. Later, with the aid of armoured formations placed at his disposal by O.K.H. he was able to counter-attack. On October 21 and 22, trying to force a passage over the River Angerapp, the 11th Guards Army was assailed from the north and south and thrown back in disorder onto the right bank of the Rominte. Chernyakhovsky left behind him 1,000-odd tanks and more than 300 guns. He also left clear traces of atrocities of all kinds committed by his troops against the inhabitants of some 300 villages. As may

▽ *Even in the forests of East Prussia the tank/infantry tactics developed by the Russians proved quite effective.*

well be imagined, Goebbels made great play with these atrocities. The result of his propaganda was that, three months later, five or six million Germans fled before the Soviet invasion, in temperatures of 20 degrees below zero.

Among the causes of the check of the Russian 3rd Belorussian Front on the Kaunas–Königsberg line should be mentioned the inability of the 2nd Belorussian Front to move out of its bridgeheads on the Narew and thus catch Hossbach in a pincer movement. This would have imitated the manoeuvre

△ △ *President R. H. Ryti of Finland inspects an artillery command post. Within a few weeks he was to be made the "scapegoat" of the breach between Finland and Russia.*
△ *Russian artillerymen with their gun behind a camouflage screen of branches.*

attempted by Samsonov as he marched to meet Rennenkampf in August 1914. Should the dismissal of General Zakharov be considered as a punishment for this lack of success? Whether or not this was the reason, at the turn of the year, General Zakharov was called upon to hand over his command to Marshal Rokossovsky.

Mannerheim called to power

In Helsinki, on August 1, acting out a previously-prepared drama, President Ryti resigned as head of state and the Finnish parliament appointed Marshal Mannerheim as his successor. This 75-year-old soldier would have to pilot the nation out of the war. For this purpose, he held a trump card in the performance of the Finnish Army during the recent battle of Karelia. So much heroism, spirit, and tenacity could effectively have shown the Kremlin that Finland's unconditional surrender could only be bought at a price much greater than any benefit that might be obtained from it. But before negotiating with Moscow, Finland could not wait for the Red Army to settle itself solidly in Tallinn and Paltiski, which would allow it to launch an amphibious operation across the Gulf of Finland and to use its crushing superiority in men and *matériel* to the best advantage.

In his task Mannerheim had to take into account the German 20th Army. This possessed three corps (ten mountain divisions) and faced Russia between the Arctic Circle and the Rybachiy peninsula on the frozen Arctic Ocean. This force, including the naval gunners in the many coastal batteries and the air force, totalled 204,000 men under the command of Colonel-General Dr. Rendulic.

The consequences of Finland's "defection" . . .

O.K.W. had envisaged the possibility of a Finnish defection since the spring. It had prepared two operations to counter-act its effects. Operation *"Birke"* (Birch tree) provided for the 20th Army to retreat on the Finno-Norwegian frontier, while Operation "*Tanne*" (Pine tree) would require the army and the navy to prepare to occupy the Åland Islands, in the south of the Gulf of Bothnia, and the island of Sur Sari or Hogland in the Gulf of Finland.

Meanwhile on June 26, with the Soviet offensive at full force in the Karelian Isthmus, Ribbentrop had agreed to supply arms to the Finns only if they bound themselves unconditionally to the Third Reich. Trapped, President Ryti, with the verbal approval of his ministers, had agreed to this in writing. Therefore his resignation could imply a tacit rejection of the signature as being put on the agreement entirely on his own responsibility. Such a subterfuge was absolutely justified in view of Germany's blackmail.

. . . and Germany's contingency plans

That was how Blücher, Germany's minister in Helsinki, and General Erfurth, O.K.W.'s liaison officer attached to Marshal Mannerheim, interpreted the crisis of August 1 and the solution adopted. Rendulic, for his part, pointed out that the Finnish Minister of War, General Walden, had made no reference to Finno-German military partnership during that interview. And so the staff of the 20th Army began to prepare Operation "*Birke*" with all speed.

To clarify the situation, Hitler sent the O.K.W. chief-of-staff to see the new President of the Finnish Republic. Keitel was received by Mannerheim on August 17 and had the arrogance or the tactlessness to tell the latter that the people of the Greater Reich would maintain their war effort for another ten years if it were necessary. This swagger was received coldly and politely with the answer that "it was probably true for a nation of 90 million people".

As may be well imagined, Mannerheim did not express his thoughts too openly. All the same, he did not conceal the fact that Ryti's resignation had come because "in view of circumstances beyond his control, the ex-President had not been able to maintain his freedom of action", and that Mannerheim himself had agreed to combine in his person the supreme military and civil power in order that "in their precarious situation the Finnish

people could rely on having the freedom to act within their own interests".

Though he put a brave face on this, Keitel did not fail for a moment to realise the meaning and the importance of these prudent statements. Mannerheim was going to begin to "guide" Finland out of the war.

Relations with Russia renewed

And, in fact, on August 25, the Soviet minister in Stockholm, Mme. Kollontai, was surprised by a message from the Finnish Government, asking her what the Soviet conditions would be for re-opening the peace talks which had been broken off on April 18 at Finland's request.

◁ *Inhabitants of Helsinki emerge from their air-raid shelters to survey the damage caused by Russian bombers.*
△ *With a raid imminent, a Finnish policeman orders pedestrians into the shelters.*
▽ *While his parents arrange transport out of the city, this Helsinki boy guards what his family have recovered from their bombed-out home.*

△ *Finnish soldiers rest in a northern town.*
▷ *Women auxiliaries of the Finnish Army in an observation post.*

▽ *Mealtime for Finnish troops at a camp staffed by young girls.*

The Soviet reply arrived at Helsinki in record time and included only two conditions:

1. Immediate breaking-off of diplomatic relations between the Republic of Finland and the Third Reich.
2. Evacuation in two weeks, the absolutely final date fixed for September 14, of all Wehrmacht forces stationed in Finnish territory, after which the Helsinki Government agreed to intern any men left behind.

Great Britain associated herself with these conditions and the United States, who had not declared war on Finland, made it known that they approved. On September 2, after a session behind locked doors, the Finnish parliament authorised the government to begin discussions on the basis of the above conditions.

In consequence there was a cease-fire between the Russians and the Finns at 0700 hours on September 5.

Mannerheim informs Hitler

As Minister Blücher was receiving his passports on September 2, Mannerheim had a handwritten letter given to General Erfurth to be passed on the Führer.

It was, Mannerheim wrote, first of all the general development of the war which "more and more prevents Germany from providing us, in the precarious situations which will doubtless arise and at the right time and in sufficient quantity, the aid of which we shall have urgent need and which Germany, as I sincerely believe, would be willing to grant us".

Moreover, if the worst occurred, the risks run by both countries, as Mannerheim told Keitel, were far from equal. Here, he added, "I must point out that even if fate did not favour German arms, Germany could continue to exist. Nobody could say the same for Finland."

And, at the same time as he heaped praises on the behaviour of "our German brothers-in-arms" towards the Finnish population, he declared that he cherished the hope that "even if you disapprove of my letter you will want, as do I and all Finns, to control the present situation and avoid any worsening of it".

However, the implementation of the second condition imposed by Moscow on Helsinki would set the Finns and Germans against each other—and for good reason, for it could not be done in the time allowed. Both Marshal Manner-heim and Colonel-General Rendulic agree on this in their memoirs.

Though XIX Mountain Corps (General Ferdinand Jodl), whose left faced the Rybachiy peninsula, could get over the Norwegian frontier in a few days' march, this did not apply to the right wing of the 20th Army, consisting of XXXVI Mountain Corps (General Vogel); in action halfway between the White Sea and the Russo-Finnish frontier in the south, in a fortnight he would have to cross a good 625 miles before he left Finnish territory. That is why, from September 3, Manner-heim began to study the means at his disposal to keep his word regarding the internment of his ex-comrades in arms.

Hitler was the first to make a move. Though he ordered Rendulic to carry on with Operation *"Birke"* and abandoned the idea of a landing on the Åland Islands for fear of possible Swedish reaction, he nevertheless maintained his decision to put Sur Sari under firm Wehrmacht control, in spite of the objections of Vice-Admiral Buchardi, commander of

the Kriegsmarine in that part of the Baltic.

The expedition was launched in the night of September 14-15 and resulted in total defeat for the Germans. Colonel Mietinnen, under whose command the island's garrison had been placed, conducted a spirited defence and then counter-attacked with such energy that the following evening the Germans had lost 330 killed and wounded, and surrendered a good 1,000 of their men.

The news of this unpardonable act of aggression and its defeat was welcomed in official circles in Helsinki with certain relief. From now on there was no need to bother about an ally of that sort.

In any case, even if Hitler had restrained himself from committing this act of brutal stupidity, events would not have taken a very different course. A few days later, it would have been known in Helsinki that Rendulic had received orders to stay in Finnish Lappland so as to keep the base at Petsamo and the precious nickel mines of Kolosjoki for the Third Reich.

△ *A member of the Russian armistice commission on the day of his arrival in Helsinki on September 22, 1944. Behind him to the left are three Swedish newspapermen.*

▽ *German soldiers in Helsinki just prior to their evacuation from the country.*

Retreat to Norway

Mannerheim now transferred his III Corps into the region of Oulu on the Gulf of Bothnia. This corps was commanded by General Siilasvuo, who had distinguished himself during the campaign of the winter of 1939-40. But the Germans did not permit a breakthrough, although their new enemies tried to cut them off by an unexpected landing at Kemi, close to the Finno-Swedish frontier.

On October 15, the Germans evacuated the little town of Rovaniemi after having reduced it to ashes. Then they slipped into Norwegian territory along the route they had prepared between Rovaniemi and Pörsangerfjord. It was difficult to pursue the retreating Germans because they methodically destroyed all bridges, and also because of the season and the fact that the Finnish Army was due to complete its demobilisation by December 5, 1944.

On October 4, O.K.W. ordered Colonel-General Rendulic to abandon Petsamo and to fall back on Lyngenfjord. His preparations for the retreat were almost complete when, on October 7, XIX Corps was attacked in great strength and most energetically by the Karelian Front troops under General K. A. Meretskov. The 20th Army met this Soviet offensive with delaying tactics, using the many rivers in the region. On October 9, XIX Corps was on the point of being surrounded but the danger was averted by the fast 400 mile transfer of the 163rd Division, which hurled itself into Salmijärvi, and then by the rest of XXXVI Mountain Corps.

Petsamo was occupied on October 15 by the Russians, who then pushed on as far as Kirkenes, on Norwegian soil. This battle, fought above the Arctic Circle, earned Meretskov the title of Marshal of the Soviet Union. In spite of this, it is strange that Soviet accounts, normally so rich in detail, make no mention of trophies or prisoners when they speak of this battle.

The Lyngenfjord base included the fjord of that name, half-way between the North Cape and Tromsö, and also the salient of Finnish territory which protrudes into the region. This meant the sacrifice of the Norwegian province of Finnmark, whose population was evacuated while the Germans burnt Lyngenfjord and Hammerfest. After its retreat, the 20th Army was dissolved. Three of its divisions were given to O.B.W., and a fourth was put at the disposal of O.K.W. Colonel-General Rendulic received the command of the "Norway" Army.

On September 19, 1944, the new Finnish minister, Enckell, was in Moscow to sign an "armistice treaty" which can be taken as a real preliminary and whose clauses regarding territory and payments

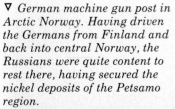

▽ German machine gun post in Arctic Norway. Having driven the Germans from Finland and back into central Norway, the Russians were quite content to rest there, having secured the nickel deposits of the Petsamo region.

were reproduced in the definitive peace treaty.

△ *Germans at work digging a trench from the frozen earth above the Arctic Circle.*

Finland's peace

In addition to the loss of territory which Finland had had to suffer by the treaty of March 7, 1940, she now had to witness the amputation of the Petsamo region, thus losing her access to the Atlantic as well as the advantages she gained through the export of nickel from Kolosjoki.

In exchange for the lease of the Hangö peninsula, which the first Treaty of Moscow had granted Russia for 50 years, in the second treaty the Soviet Union obtained the same rights over the Porkala promontory on the Gulf of Finland, less than 25 miles from Helsinki.

Out of a population of four million, the valiant little nation had lost 55,000 dead and 47,500 wounded.

CHAPTER 134
Defeat in the Balkans

On August 20, 1944, the troops of the 2nd Ukrainian Front attacked Iaşi, capital of Moldavia. On Christmas Eve, acting in concert with the 3rd Ukrainian Front, it laid siege to Budapest, while the Soviet Union took complete control over Bulgaria. It exercised no less strong an influence over those provinces of Yugoslavia liberated by Marshal Tito, as well as over the ex-kingdom of Albania.

Not only had the "New Order" instituted by Hitler and Mussolini been upset, but also the old European balance, established in these parts in the 19th Century. On June 22, 1944, Army Group "South Ukraine", which had responsibility for the 400-mile front running between the mouth of the Danube and the Carpathian range, included 23 Rumanian and 33 German divisions, nine of which were Panzer or *Panzergrenadier*. But the defeat in Belorussia, the rout in the western Ukraine, and the invasion of Poland had forced O.K.H. to remove six Panzer and seven infantry divisions from this army group. They had only been partially replaced by units of lesser worth. With everything included, when Colonel-General Hans Friessner succeeded Schörner at the head of Army Group "South Ukraine" at the beginning of August, he took over 52 divisions, 24 of which were German. What made the circumstances more serious was that he had only four Panzer divisions.

Antonescu recommends retreat

It had become evident that the Russians had two formidable bridgeheads on the Dniestr, at Tiraspol and Grigoriopol, and that between the Dniestr and the Prut the position of the front favoured one of those pincer movements so liked by the Russians. So Marshal Antonescu, the Rumanian *Conducator,* summoned to

◁ *Cheerful Rumanian musicians welcome the Russians to Rumania.*
▽ ◁ *The Axis begins to dissolve. The* St. Paul Dispatch *of Minnesota poses the pertinent question 'Who'll jump first?' It was in fact to be Finland, closely followed by Rumania and then Bulgaria.*
▽ *German comment on the "liquidation" of the Axis satellites. Stalin, as auctioneer, offers: "Here's another lot of little countries: Rumania, Bulgaria, and Finland. No one wants them? I'll take them then . . ."*

Cossack cavalry move up through a Rumanian village, to the apparent delight of its inhabitants.

O.K.W. on August 5, offered as his advice that Army Group "South Ukraine" should be pulled back along a line running from the northern arm of the Danube, through Galaţi to the right bank of the Siretul and then the Carpathians. This line had been surveyed and partially fortified by the Belgian General Brialmont at a time when fear of the Russians had caused Rumania to flirt with the Triple Alliance. Strategically sound, this solution nevertheless required the evacuation of the southern districts of Bessarabia and Moldavia, a serious sacrifice for Rumania that Antonescu nevertheless made.

Rumanian peace overtures

The day after the last interview between the Führer and Antonescu, the latter summoned Colonel-General Guderian to go over the political and military scene with him. Guderian wrote:

"He soon came to talk about the assassination attempt of July 20, without hiding his horror at it. 'Believe me,' he said, 'I could trust any of my generals with my life. In Rumania, it would be inconceivable for any officer to take part in a *coup d'état!*' There and then, I was not in a position to answer his grave reproaches. A fortnight later, Antonescu would find himself in a very different situation, and so should we."

It seems, therefore, that the Rumanian dictator had not the slightest idea of the plot led by King Michael I and the leaders of the main political parties, who were preparing to seize power from his hands. As was seen earlier, following the battle of Stalingrad, Rumanian diplomats had attempted to re-establish contact with Great Britain and the United States. In 1944, Alexander Creziano, the Rumanian minister in Ankara, contacted the representatives of the two Western powers while the embassies in Madrid and Stockholm went forward with other soundings. Finally, with the consent of the King, the leader of the National Peasants' Party, Julius Maniu, who was the principal conspirator, sent two emissaries to Cairo in the persons of

Constantin Visoïano and Prince Stirbey.
But neither Washington nor London was
disposed to reply to these overtures before
Bucharest had reached agreement with
Moscow on the conditions for a cease-fire.

Now, on April 2, Antonescu's adver-
saries noted a statement by Molotov that
they interpreted as an encouraging over-
ture.

"The Soviet Union," proclaimed
Stalin's Foreign Minister, "in no
way seeks to acquire any part of
Rumanian territory or to change the
present social order. Russian troops have
entered Rumania solely as a result of
military necessity."

Certainly, when Molotov spoke of
"Rumanian territory", he excluded the
provinces of Bessarabia and Bukovina,
which the ultimatum of June 26, 1940
had placed under Soviet control. All the
same, Julius Maniu informed the Allies
that he was ready to enter discussions
on this basis and to consent to substantial reparations being paid to Moscow. It is also true that Rumania had
been assured that, as soon as she left the
German camp, she would be able to get
back the part of Transylvania that the
Vienna agreement of August 30, 1940 had
transferred to Hungary.

The Rumanian dictator was more or

▽ *The Rumanian high
command: King Michael
(bare-headed, in the background)
and Marshal Antonescu
(bare-headed, in the foreground).
Soon afterwards, a coup
headed by King Michael ousted
Antonescu and threw
Rumania's lot in with the
Allies.*

The German Panzerjäger IV/70 tank destroyer

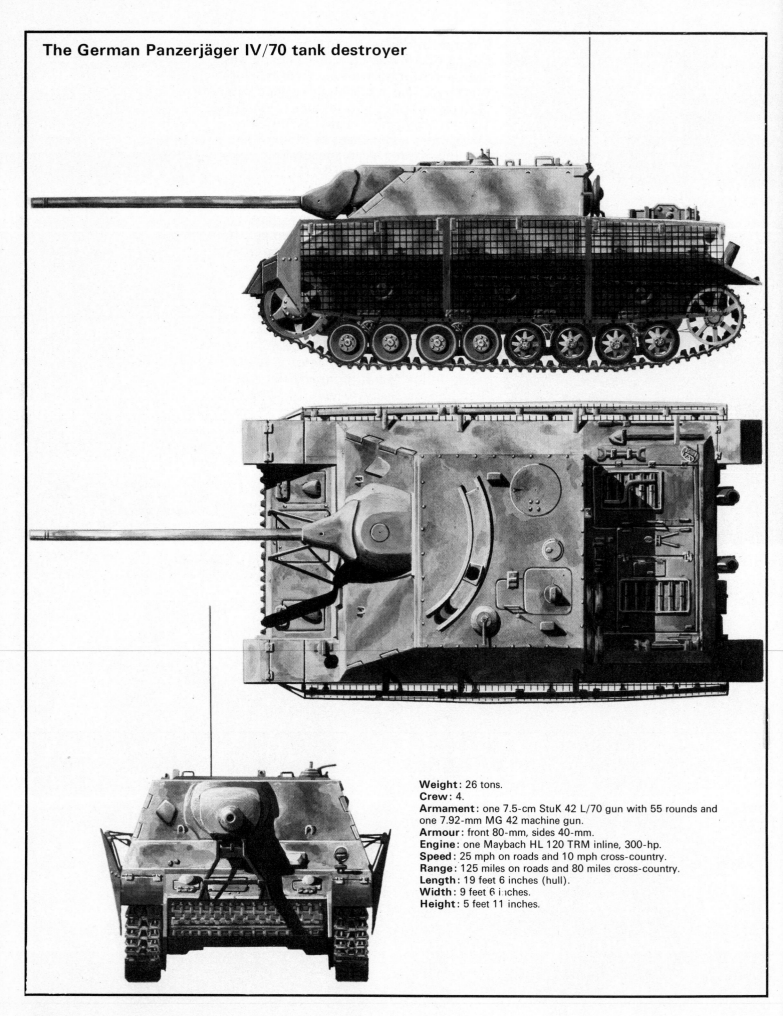

Weight: 26 tons.
Crew: 4.
Armament: one 7.5-cm StuK 42 L/70 gun with 55 rounds and one 7.92-mm MG 42 machine gun.
Armour: front 80-mm, sides 40-mm.
Engine: one Maybach HL 120 TRM inline, 300-hp.
Speed: 25 mph on roads and 10 mph cross-country.
Range: 125 miles on roads and 80 miles cross-country.
Length: 19 feet 6 inches (hull).
Width: 9 feet 6 inches.
Height: 5 feet 11 inches.

less aware of these dealings, but did not forbid them absolutely. He merely refused to agree to them, considering that his honour bound him to the Wehrmacht. Moreover, he did not feel personally threatened, ignoring the fact that it was not to him but to the sovereign that the officer corps had sworn loyalty.

The Rumanian situation caused great puzzlement in Hitler's circle for the reports being received were in disagreement with each other.

On August 3, Friessner had sounded the alarm and indicated how little confidence he felt in his Rumanian subordinates, particularly the senior officers. Hence his conclusion:

"If these symptoms of insecurity among the Rumanian troops go on being noted for long, it will be necessary to order an immediate retreat on the front behind the Prut on the Galati–Focşani–Carpathians line."

But General Hansen, who had been the "German General in Rumania" since October 1940, held a diametrically opposed opinion. The representative of the Third Reich in Bucharest, Ambassador von Killinger, telegraphed Ribbentrop on August 10: "Situation absolutely stable. King Michael guarantees the alliance with Germany."

Certainly this diplomat was not very highly thought of by Ribbentrop, but Marshal Antonescu had the entire con-

△ *Russian air superiority. With the few Axis aircraft left swept out of the skies by Russian fighters (the patrol is composed of Lavochkin La-5's), Soviet close support aircraft could blast open a path for the tanks and infantry.*

◁ *Russian armour moves into Bucharest in August 1944 to the acclaim of the Rumanian public.*

fidence of Hitler. That is why, in view of Hitler's optimism, nothing was prepared by the Germans to ease the consequences of a "defection".

Rumanian collapse

On the vital day, that is at dawn on August 20, Army Group "South Ukraine" was divided into two sections:

1. From the Black Sea to Korneshty, *Armeegruppe* "Dumitrescu" included the Rumanian 3rd Army (General Dumitrescu) and the German 6th Army (General Fretter-Pico).
2. From Korneshty to the Yablonitse pass (contact on the right with Army Group "North Ukraine") *Armeegruppe* "Wöhler" put the German 8th Army (General Wöhler) and the Rumanian 4th Army (General Steflea) into the field.

So, of 250 miles of front, 100 were

defended by Rumanian troops but, for reasons of security, "integration" as it is now called, of the Axis forces had gone as far as army level and, in some places, down to corps level. The system, which in his jargon Hitler had curiously named "whalebone stays", was at its height here. It was–ignoring for the moment the plans of King Michael and the suspicions of Colonel-General Friessner–to ignore the wisdom of the old saying that a chain is only as strong as its weakest link.

As usual, the Soviet sources say nothing of the numbers of men which the *Stavka* put at the disposal of Generals Malinovsky and Tolbukhin; the Germans, for their part, calculate them as 90 or 94 infantry divisions and seven tank corps. In armoured strength alone, this gave the attackers an advantage of at least five to one. In his centre of gravity, which pivoted on Iaşi, Malinovsky had massed 125 guns and mortars per mile. Tolbukhin's advance from the Tiraspol

bridgehead was, in addition, aided by 7,800 guns. Soviet aircraft dominated the skies and, during the preparation of the attack, the Red Air Force co-operated with the artillery in attacking enemy positions, then transferred its effort along the lines taken by the Germans' reserve armour.

By the evening of August 20, both Malinovsky and Tolbukhin had already gained victory. In the German 8th Army, IV Corps (General Mieth) resisted fiercely in the outskirts of Iaşi, but the Rumanian IV Corps on its left foundered in spite of the help of the 76th Division. *Armeegruppe* "Dumitrescu" had been attacked at the link-point between the German 6th Army and the Rumanian 3rd Army, and the rupture was even more decisive after the collapse of the two Rumanian divisions which completed General Brandenberger's XXIX Corps. And while the Russians followed up their advantage, Friessner had already used up his ar-

The original caption reads: "The watch on the Danube. Two major tasks have devolved on the Hungarian Army, which is excellently trained and superbly equipped: first the protection of Hungary against foreign threats and occupation; second, by preserving her independence the ensuring of free trade between Central and South-Eastern Europe, between Greater Germany and the Balkan States. This trade, whose main route is the Danube, forms the basis of the New Order in Europe." And it was all crumbling in the autumn of 1944.
◁ Gunboats on the Danube.
△ A.A. guns.

moured reserves (13th Panzer Division, 10th *Panzergrenadier* Division, and Rumanian 1st Armoured Division).

In this situation, there was nothing Friessner could do but take the responsibility himself of ordering his army group to retreat without waiting for Hitler's authorisation. He did so that same evening. But, as he himself remarked:

"In spite of the preparations we had made in more leisurely moments, we were naturally unable to disengage ourselves from the enemy methodically. The way the situation was developing, any movement of ours could only be carried out under the enemy's control and only step by step. This was not now a retreat, it was a fighting withdrawal."

▽ *Sofia welcomes the Red Army. On the banner is the slogan "Death to Fascism".*
▽▽ *The Red Navy moves into the Bulgarian Black Sea base of Varna.*

Antonescu overthrown

The *Führerbefehl* reached Friessner on August 22. The following day King Michael summoned Antonescu and his Minister of Foreign Affairs to the palace and ordered them to conclude an immediate armistice with the Allies. The Marshal's reply was vague, and the King immediately had them both arrested. Then, at 2200 hours, Radio Bucharest broadcast the cease-fire order to all Rumanian forces. When the commander of Army Group "South Ukraine" heard the news, he rang up Generals Dumitrescu and Steflea. Both men refused to disobey the oath of loyalty they had sworn to their sovereign. At the same time, Ambassador von Killinger and General Hansen were confined to the German legation.

Hitler was totally surprised by this turn of events and, without even warning Friessner of his intentions, ordered Luftwaffe formations based on Ploieşti to bomb Bucharest, concentrating particularly on the Royal Palace and the Prime Minister's residence. This was a particularly stupid thing to do and the new Prime Minister, General Sanatescu, took advantage of it to declare war on the Third Reich on August 25. As a result, Rumanian troops occupied the Danube, Prut, and Siretul crossings, opening them to the Russians.

6th Army routed

This was followed by a complete disaster for the German 6th Army. Cut off from the Danube by Tolbukhin's armour, which had pushed through as far as the Prut at Leovo, it could not cross the river higher up because that would have thrown it into the arms of Malinovsky, whose 6th Guards Tank Army (Colonel-General Chistyakov) had pushed on swiftly from Iaşi towards Huşi. Fourteen German divisions were annihilated in the pincers thus formed, and only two divisional commanders escaped death or capture. All four corps commanders were taken prisoner. In the German 8th Army, IV Corps, which had retreated along the right bank of the Prut, was trapped by the Russian 2nd Ukrainian Front, and the remains of its 79th and 376th Divisions were forced to lay down their arms with their commanders, Lieutenant-Generals Weinknecht and Schwarz. General Mieth did not suffer the same humiliation, having succumbed in the meantime to a heart attack. To sum up, of 24 German divisions which he had under his command on August 20, Colonel-General Friessner had lost 16 in the space of a fortnight. The Soviet communiqué of September 5 claimed 105,000 German dead and 106,000 prisoners.

The right course?

Seeing their country subjected to the Communist yoke and enslaved to the U.S.S.R., certain emigré Rumanians see the events of August 23 as the cause of their country's unfortunate fate. In this they do not appear to be correct. In the

△ ◁ *Back in the Reich, all production records for armaments were being smashed as Speer's production plan swung into full speed. Here production workers finish off a batch of 3.7-cm anti-aircraft guns.*

△ *Bulgarian partisans prepare for an ambush on the retreating Germans.*

U.S.S.R., Great Britain, and the U.S.A., but was the only one to sign. What was more serious was that, while Ambassador Bogomolov sat as an equal partner in the organisation charged with carrying out the Italian armistice, the Allied commission set up by Article 18 of that agreement, with the same rôle, had its activity strictly limited; it read:

"The Allied Commission will follow the instructions of the Soviet High Command (Allied) acting in the name of the Allied Powers."

On the military side, it is also worth noting that the armistice of September 12 obliged Rumania to declare war on Germany and Hungary and pursue it with a minimum of 12 divisions, placed under the "Soviet High Command (Allied)". But already, on September 6, the Bucharest Government had declared war against Hungary.

And so it was as on a peace-time route march that Marshal Malinovsky sent 25 divisions of his front from Wallachia to Transylvania, while his left marched towards Turnu Severin on the frontier with Yugoslavia. By September 1, Tolbukhin had reached Giurgiu on the Danube.

The Rumanian cease-fire raised the

first place the destruction caused by the war on land stopped at the left bank of the Danube and the Siretul and the cease-fire saved the lives of hundreds of thousands of young Rumanians, for the battle for Moldavia and Bessarabia was already irrevocably lost, and in the worst conditions.

It is also evident that neither King Michael nor those who had advised him could imagine that they would be purely and simply abandoned to the Communist subversion ordered from a distance by Moscow. Having re-established the liberal constitution of 1921, restored political rights, and freed political prisoners, they counted on being granted the benefits of the Atlantic Charter of August 14, 1941 and the principles it had proclaimed in the face of Hitler.

But the fatal process was already under way. The Rumanian emissaries who had arrived in Cairo were sent to Moscow. The British and Americans agreed to appear in the background in the armistice agreement, which was signed on September 12 between King Michael's plenipotentiaries and Marshal Malinovsky, who spoke for the governments of the

question of Bulgaria. The situation in Sofia was as follows. On December 12, 1941 King Boris had declared war against the United States and Great Britain but, for historical reasons, had been careful not to engage in hostilities against the Soviet Union. On his mysterious death, which occurred on August 28, 1943 after a visit to Hitler, a Regency Council, composed of his brother Prince Cyril, Professor Filov, and General Michov, assumed power in the name of King Simon II, who was only a child.

It was thus logical that the Regents should send a delegation to Cairo to enquire about the armistice conditions that London and Washington might be willing to grant them. At the same time they formed a democratic-style government and denounced the Anti-Comintern Pact, which Bulgaria had joined on November 25, 1941.

These peaceful overtures were received by Stalin, on September 5, by a declaration of war. The Bulgarian Government thought it could counter this by declaring war against Germany on September 8. For the Kremlin the important point was to bring the negotiations to Moscow and exclude the British and the Americans. The signing of the armistice took place in Moscow on October 28 and General Maitland Wilson, commander-in-chief of the Allied forces in the Mediterranean, was reduced to the rôle of a mere spectator. Meanwhile, forces of the 3rd Ukrainian Front had penetrated Bulgaria at Silistra and Ruse, amid popular acclaim. Several days later the Gheorghiev government, preponderantly Communist, was formed. Soon the reign of terror began in Bulgaria. Dismissed, imprisoned, dragged before a carefully selected court, all three Regents fell before a firing squad on February 2, 1945. They were naked, as a diplomat at the time posted to Sofia recounted later, because the authorities wanted to preserve their clothes.

Following the declaration of war on September 8, Bulgaria sent its 5th Army against Germany. It was commanded by General Stanchev and had ten divisions equipped by the Wehrmacht, including one armoured division which had just received 88 Pzkw IV tanks and 50 assault guns. Acting as Marshal Tolbukhin's left wing, it was given the task of cutting the Germans' line of retreat as they pulled back from the Balkans. It was only partially successful in this, as we shall see in the next chapter.

△ *Julius Maniu, head of the Rumanian National Peasants' Party.*

▽ *The signing of the Russo-Bulgarian armistice on October 24, 1944. Foreign Minister Molotov is standing seventh from the right.*

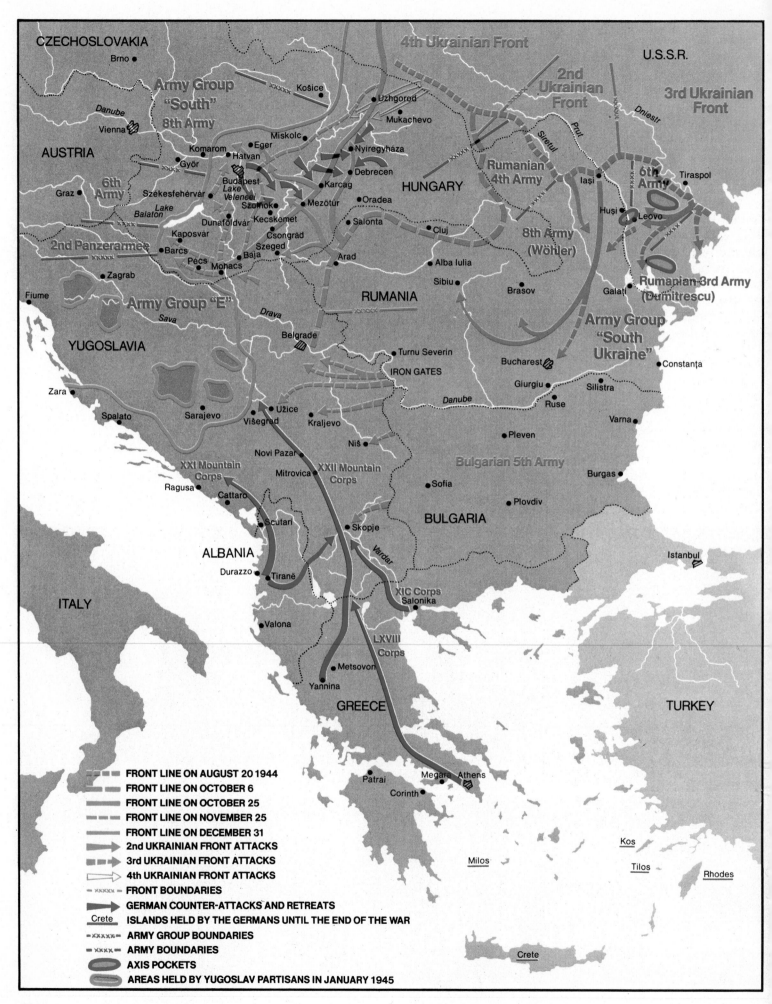

CZECHOSLOVAKIA

Brno

4th Ukrainian Front

U.S.S.R.

Army Group "South" 8th Army

Košice

Vienna

Danube

AUSTRIA

Uzhgorod

Mukachevo

2nd Ukrainian Front

3rd Ukrainian Front

Dniestr

Komárom

Eger

Miskolc

Nyiregyháza

Tiraspol

Graz

6th Army

Győr

Hatvan

Debrecen

Karcag

HUNGARY

Rumanian 4th Army

Iași

6th Army

Székesfehérvár

Budapest

Lake Velencei

Mezőtúr

Oradea

Cluj

Huşi

Leovo

Lake Balaton

Szolnok

Kecskemét

Salonta

8th Army (Wöhler)

2nd Panzerarmee

Kaposvár

Dunaföldvár

Csongrád

Arad

Alba Iulia

Galaţi

Rumanian 3rd Army (Dumitrescu)

Pécs

Baja

Sibiu

Brasov

Zagreb

Barcs

Mohacs

RUMANIA

Army Group "South Ukraine"

Fiume

Army Group "E"

Drava

Belgrade

Bucharest

Constanţa

Sava

YUGOSLAVIA

Turnu Severin

IRON GATES

Giurgiu

Silistra

Zara

Danube

Ruse

Varna

Spalato

Sarajevo

Užice

Pleven

Višegrad

Kraljevo

Niš

Novi Pazar

Burgas

XXI Mountain Corps

Mitrovica

XXII Mountain Corps

Bulgarian 5th Army

Ragusa

Cattaro

Sofia

Plovdiv

Scutari

Skopje

BULGARIA

ALBANIA

Vardar

Durazzo

Tiranë

XIC Corps

Salonika

Istanbul

ITALY

Valona

LXVIII Corps

Metsovon

Yannina

GREECE

TURKEY

Patrai

Megara Athens

Corinth

Kos

Milos

Tilos

Rhodes

Crete

FRONT LINE ON AUGUST 20 1944
FRONT LINE ON OCTOBER 6
FRONT LINE ON OCTOBER 25
FRONT LINE ON NOVEMBER 25
FRONT LINE ON DECEMBER 31
2nd UKRAINIAN FRONT ATTACKS
3rd UKRAINIAN FRONT ATTACKS
4th UKRAINIAN FRONT ATTACKS
FRONT BOUNDARIES
GERMAN COUNTER-ATTACKS AND RETREATS
ISLANDS HELD BY THE GERMANS UNTIL THE END OF THE WAR
ARMY GROUP BOUNDARIES
ARMY BOUNDARIES
AXIS POCKETS
AREAS HELD BY YUGOSLAV PARTISANS IN JANUARY 1945

CHAPTER 135
Confusion in the Balkans

On August 23, the German forces occupying Albania, mainland Greece, and the Aegean Islands came under Colonel-General Löhr, commanding Army Group "E" with headquarters at Salonika. These forces were subdivided into four corps (Tiranë, Yanina, Athens, and Salonika) totalling ten divisions (seven of which were on the mainland) and six fortress brigades: in all, about 300,000 men, to whom must be added 33,000 sailors (most of whom were attached to the coastal artillery) and 12,000 airmen and anti-aircraft gunners.

The day following the Rumanian cease-fire, Löhr was confronted by an order from O.K.W. ordering him to begin evacuation of the Aegean and Ionian islands and mainland Greece, south of a line running from Corfu to Métsovon and Mt. Olympus. But a few days later Sofia's declaration of war on Berlin forced Hitler to annul this order and to instruct Army Group "E" to retreat to a line running along the line Scutari–Skopje–Bulgarian/Yugoslav frontier of 1939–Iron Gate Pass on the Danube. On the other side of the river he would be in contact with the 2nd *Panzerarmee* (General de Angelis). The latter would relieve Field-Marshal von Weichs's Army Group "F". In this way a continuous front between the Carpathians and the Adriatic would be formed to bar the enemy from the Danube plain.

Time was pressing, and it was not possible to recover all the 60,000 men who garrisoned the Aegean. Using the very few transport aircraft available and a large number of powered *caiques,* two-thirds of the men were brought back to mainland Greece. The remainder continued to hold Rhodes, Léros, Kos, and Tílos under the command of Major-General Wagner, as well as Crete and the island of Mílos under General Benthak. They remained there until after the end of the war on May 9, 1945.

The evacuation of the Peloponnese gave rise to some clashes between the 41st Division (Lieutenant-General Hauser) and the royalist guerrillas of Napoleon Zervas, opportunely reinforced by the British 2nd Airborne Brigade, which liberated Patras on October 4. All the same, the Germans reached Corinth, then Athens which General Felmy, commanding LXVIII Corps, handed over to the control of its mayor that same day. In Epiros, the troops of XXII Mountain Corps (General Lanz) fought bitter battles

As the Red Army moved deeper into the Balkans, the uneasy anti-Axis truce between the Royalists and the Communists in Greece broke down completely. The latter, in the hope of securing Russian intervention in Greece, started an insurrection in Athens. But Greece fell within the British sphere of influence, and Churchill reacted swiftly. Comprising airborne landings and subsequent amphibious reinforcement, Operation "Manna" was intended to nip the Communist flower in the bud. But soon General Scobie's III Corps found itself embroiled in a full scale civil war.
▽ *British paratroopers in Athens during the E.L.A.S. uprising. Note the weapons carried: a Bren gun, an American M1 carbine, and an American Thompson sub-machine gun.*

with partisans. But, all in all, the evacuation of Greece took place with very few losses and serious delays to the retreating Germans.

Mention should be made here that in 1947, the Greek Government revealed to the United Nations the text of an agreement made between a representative of the 11th Luftwaffe Division and a delegate of the "E.L.A.S." partisans, according to whose terms the men of the "Peoples' Army" agreed not to hinder the German retreat on the condition that they were given a certain quantity of heavy arms and other military equipment for their forthcoming war with the loyalists.

Trouble in Yugoslavia

It was in Yugoslavia that things became difficult for Army Group "E". On October 14, the Bulgarian 5th Army took Niš, on the most practical route for the Germans to reach the Danube. In addition, on October 1, Tolbukhin had crossed the Danube near Turnu Severin and then forced his way over the Morava against the resistance of XXXIV Corps' (General F. W. Müller) two divisions. Then the Russians marched on Belgrade. On October 20, working with Marshal Tito's troops, they overcame the final resistance in the streets of the Yugoslav capital, undertaken by *Armeegruppe "Felber"* (Army Group "F").

The fall of Niš had forced Löhr to think of a way to escape the noose and he decided to follow a route through Skopje, Mitrovica, Novi Pazar, and Višegrad. The Belgrade road would have enabled Tolbukhin to cut Army Group "E"'s last line of retreat if his enemy had not opportunely guarded his flanks around Kraljevo and Užice. In short, Colonel-General Löhr established his headquarters at Sarajevo on November 15, having managed to bring his four corps through

◁ ◁ *E.L.A.S. supporters on the roof of Athens University.*
▽ ◁ *Male and female soldiers of E.L.A.S. With the Germans pulling back towards Yugoslavia, E.L.A.S. now saw its task as leading Greece into the Communist bloc.*
▽ *Loyalists demonstrate in favour of Papandreou and the Western Allies.*

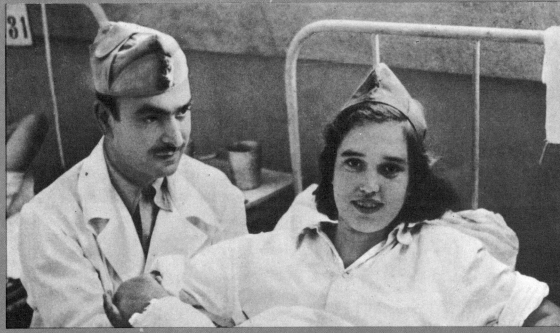

▷ *Doctor Carlo Ubertalli tends Ksenija Kavacic, an 18-year old Yugoslav partisan wounded in an attack on the German-held town of Klis. She finally arrived in Italy for hospital treatment under the care of Doctor Ubertalli, who had sent the partisans medical supplies while serving with the Italian Army and then deserted to the Titoist side.*

▽ *After recovering from their wounds at a hospital in Italy, these Yugoslav partisans are undergoing battle drill before being returned to Yugoslavia.*

without being encircled. Marshal Tito's Yugoslav partisans had failed in their attempts to hinder the retreat of Army Group "E" for long enough to allow Tolbukhin to develop his manoeuvre. All the same the partisans sowed hostility behind the Germans' backs in Bosnia and Hercegovina and increased their activities in Croatia and Slovenia. On the Adriatic Coast they liberated Cattaro (Kotor), Ragusa (Dubrovnik), and Spalato (Split) and, on November 8, occupied the Italian town of Zara (Zadar), which would be "slavicised" by means which Hitler would not have disdained.

Churchill pressures Bulgaria

As has been mentioned, on October 4 a British airborne force had helped to liberate Patras. A few days later, other parachute forces dropped on the aerodromes at Elevsís and Mégara. On October 14, a mixed Greek and British squadron under Rear-Admiral Troubridge dropped anchor in the Piraeus and disembarked most of the British III Corps under the command of Lieutenant-General Ronald M. Scobie.

This operation, code-named "Manna", had two aims. Following the terms of the armistice, the Bulgarian Government had agreed to return to the borders of April 6, 1941. But although Tito and Gheorghiev reached immediate understanding, the Bulgarian leader cherished the hope of being able to keep the Greek provinces of Western Thrace and Eastern Macedonia within Communist Bulgaria. These provinces had been granted to King Boris by Hitler. Here he knew he could count on the aid of E.L.A.S. (Greek Peoples' Liberation Army).

Communist *coup* prevented

Furthermore, General Scobie was ordered to prevent, by force if need be, the Peoples' Liberation Army from overturning the established system in Greece by absolutely unconstitutional means. The personality of the prime minister, George Papandreou, gave this régime a liberal, democratic, and social hue to which it was difficult to object. But the danger of

subversion was growing day by day and, summoned by a Liberation Committee of Communist inspiration (E.A.M.), units of E.L.A.S. converged on Athens, passing the retreating Germans without clashing.

In spite of the reservations of the White House and the State Department, and the furious onslaughts of the Labour M.P.s Emmanuel Shinwell and Aneurin Bevan, the cold disapproval of *The Times* and the *Manchester Guardian*, everybody knows that Churchill did not hesitate to oppose force with force without heed for his own person. Nevertheless, it was the beginning of a civil war. It would be waged savagely until the day in June 1948 when the quarrel broke between Tito and Moscow. Deprived of the important aid that Tito provided, the insurrection wavered and then collapsed under the blows struck at it in the following year by Marshal Papagos.

Malinovsky slows down

Marshal Malinovsky was last seen crossing the Wallachian Carpathians and establishing his front along the Braşov–Sibiu–Alba Iulia line. Doubtless his intention was to push straight on north and to strike the German 8th Army in the rear. This German army had established itself along the Moldavian Carpathians. But Colonel-General Friessner foresaw Malinovsky's plan, and counter-attacked from near Cluj (known then as Koloszvar) in a southerly direction, with the Hun-

△ *Churchill during his lightning visit to Athens on February 14, 1945. Later he wrote: "Only seven weeks before I had left the Greek capital rent by street-fighting. We now drove into it in an open car, where only a thin line of kilted Greek soldiers held back a vast mob, screaming with enthusiasm, in the very streets where hundreds of men had died in the Christmas days when I had last seen the city."*

Am Ende steht der Sieg!

Guards Army plunged into it and though Friessner had received five divisions as reinforcements, two from Field-Marshal von Weichs and three from O.K.H., he could not stop Malinovsky establishing himself along a line from Oradea (Nagyvárad) through Arad to Timişoara. And so, on Rumanian soil, was fought the prologue to the battle of Hungary.

The fact that, in this duel between the 2nd Ukrainian Front and the German Army Group "South", Malinovsky needed four attempts and the aid of Tolbukhin to overcome the Axis forces, when the superiority of forces was entirely to his advantage, speaks highly for the tactical ability of the German command and the standard of training of its officers and men. At the beginning of October, with his right to the south of Timişoara and his left on the Carpathians, Colonel-General Friessner could present a line between plains and mountains composed of the following:

1. Hungarian 3rd Army (General Heszlenyi);
2. German 6th Army (General Fretter-Pico); and
3. *Armeegruppe* "Wöhler", with the Hungarian 2nd Army and the German 8th Army.

In all there were nine corps and 26 divisions or their equivalent. True, they were at half their establishment strength. But IV Panzer Corps and the 24th Panzer Division would join the force shortly.

Tank clashes

One important point was that in this force there were 14 Hungarian divisions, whose combat performance caused the commander of Army Group "South" some anxiety.

On October 6, the 2nd Ukrainian Front went over to the offensive towards the north-west and the west, and attacked Salonta and south of Arad with the 6th Guards Tank Army and the 53rd and 46th Armies, whose seven tank and mechanised corps gave considerable impetus to the attack. Under the impact, the Hungarian 3rd Army broke, confirming the most pessimistic estimates of Colonel-General Friessner. Even before night had fallen, the Russians were fanning out over the Hungarian plain, some towards Debrecen, some towards Szolnok or Szeged across the Tisza.

garian 2nd Army (General Veress) and III Panzer Corps (General Breith), which had just been attached to his command. He was able to pull his 8th Army out of the Szecklers salient. In spite of this, a breach was opened between the right of the Army Group "South" (ex-"South Ukraine") and the left of Army Group "F". This breach was weakly held by the Hungarian IV and VII Corps. The 6th

Yet the Soviet tanks hurled themselves ahead to exploit their success at a speed that the infantry could not match. Furthermore, the mostly treeless Hungarian plain allowed the Panzers, as in North Africa, to adopt "warship" tactics and seek out the flanks and rear of enemy columns which kept to the roads. On the outskirts of Debrecen on October 10 the 6th Guards Tank Army was trapped in such a manoeuvre by III Panzer Corps while, on its left, the Soviet 27th Army was itself violently halted in front of Mezötúr and Karcag.

8th Army escapes

In spite of these obstacles, Malinovsky took Debrecen on October 20 and thus, on the 22nd, the armoured group under General Pliev managed to thrust 47 miles into the Tokay vineyards on the left bank of the Tisza. He profited little by it, for he was caught in a pincer from the east and the west near Myregihaza.

On October 30, an O.K.W. communiqué claimed that Malinovsky had lost close on 12,000 killed and 6,662 prisoners, and suffered the destruction or capture of about 1,000 tanks and more than 900 guns. But the losses of the German 6th Army, the temporary victors, were not small. Its six Panzer divisions now had no more than 67 tanks and 57 assault guns.

It was by paying this price that Friessner had checked Malinovsky for the second time in his attempt to cut off the retreat of the German 8th Army and to drive it into a corner in the Carpathians. Now it could align itself on the west bank of the Tisza, with the 6th Army. Following hard behind it, Colonel-General Petrov's 4th Ukrainian Front penetrated the ancient Czech province of Ruthenia. On October 26, it occupied Mukachevo and the day after, Uzhgorod.

Hungarian armistice

In spite of the occupation of Hungary, Admiral Horthy had managed to maintain his secret contacts with the British and Americans. As the situation grew worse he was obliged to give way to the demands of London and Washington, who directed him towards the Soviet Union. And so,

С НОВЫМ ГОДОМ!

at the end of September, Lieutenant-Marshal Farago, once a military attaché in Moscow, slipped away from the watching eye of the Gestapo and arrived in the Russian capital. He was, Horthy tells us, authorised to conclude an armistice, if possible under the following conditions:

"Immediate cessation of hostilities. The British and Americans to share in the occupation of Hungary. Unhindered re-

△ *The other side of the coin: a Russian poster bids the "Fascist rabble" a Happy New Year with the cheering thought that this last year of the war would see the Germans so hard pressed that they would not even be able to bury their dead.*

treat of German troops."

And so, on October 11, a preliminary armistice agreement received the signature of both parties. Did Stalin mean to press matters so as to place a *fait accompli* before the Western powers while Washington, through Churchill and Eden (then on a visit to Moscow), protested against being left out of the negotiations?

This is the version that Horthy gives in his memoirs. Eden's contain no suggestion of any such procedure. And Churchill, on October 12, 1944, telegraphed to his colleagues:

"As it is the Soviet armies which are obtaining control of Hungary, it would be natural that a major share of influence should rest with them, subject of course to an agreement with Great Britain and probably the United States, who, though not actually operating in Hungary, must view it as a Central European and not a Balkan State."

From this it is clear that Great Britain, and more so the United States, took little interest in the negotiations in course between Budapest and Moscow.

Meanwhile Admiral Horthy reached full agreement with the Prime Minister, Lakatos, and, at one in the afternoon of October 15, proclaimed an armistice in a broadcast over Budapest radio.

This broadcast was a complete condemnation of Hitler and his policies, and concluded:

"Today for everyone who can see plainly, Germany has lost the war. All governments responsible for the fate of their countries must draw their conclusions from this fact, for, as was said once by the great German statesman Bismarck: 'No nation is forced by its obligations to sacrifice itself on the altar of an alliance.'"

▽ *Russian armour races across the Hungarian* puszta. *Outnumbered and pressed steadily backwards, all that the German armoured divisions could do was to inflict the occasional heavy tactical reverses on the Russians.*
▷ *Otto Skorzeny, in the uniform of an S.S.* Hauptsturmführer *or Captain. It was this daring and resourceful man who had led the raid to rescue Mussolini, and he was now called upon to abduct the wavering Horthy.*

Skorzeny's raid

But the secret of the Hungarian-Soviet negotiations had leaked out and Hitler could count on the complicity of the Hungarian Nazis. Everything was ready for a strike. Led by the Ministers Rahn and Weesenmayer, the *Waffen*-S.S. General von dem Bach-Zalewski, and Colonel Skorzeny, it took place with lightning speed. Admiral Horthy was kidnapped in his mansion in Buda and taken under escort to the castle of Weilheim, close to Munich.

Major Szálasi, leader of the "Arrow Cross", was summoned to replace him, but in spite of his fanaticism and his ferocity, it was beyond his powers to breathe new life into the Hungarian Army. General Vörös, the chief-of-staff,

△ *Two Soviet infantrymen, armed with PPS M1943 sub-machine guns, cover three of their comrades during the street fighting for Budapest.*

surrendered at Malinovsky's headquarters. So did General Miklos, commander of the 1st Army and Louis Veress, the latter in the motor car which Guderian had just given him. It is interesting to note that during the rule of the "brown" quisling government in Budapest, a "red" quisling government was organised at Debrecen.

Malinovsky rolls on

The fall of Szeged around October 10 had forced Friessner to organise a defence line between the Tisza at Csongrád and the Danube at Baja, where he was in contact with Army Group "F". This sector was evidently the weakest, and thus it was here that Malinovsky transferred his 6th Guards Tank Army. On October 29, the 6th reopened the offensive. Its attack was directed on the Hungarian 3rd Army, which broke like a reed and opened the road to Budapest to three Soviet tank corps. In one single movement, they reached Kecskemét, only 40 miles from the capital.

But Friessner and Fretter-Pico did not lose a moment in preparing their defence.

In the Budapest bridgeheads III Panzer Corps repelled the attackers and, at the same time, the *"Feldherrnhalle" Panzergrenadier* Division (Colonel Pape) with the four Panzer divisions of LVII Panzer Corps (General Kirchner) caught the enemy columns in the flank as they moved out of Cegléd. The Russians were better organised than before, and held their ground everywhere except between Debrecen and Nyiregyháza. Moreover, the defection of the Hungarian troops in the centre and on the left of the German 6th Army allowed them to obtain several bridgeheads on the west bank of the Tisza. Even so, Malinovsky had to regroup his forces for the drive which, he hoped, would finish the business.

Germans exhausted

The Germans were nearing the end of their tether. There were very few infantry battalions which could muster 200 men. The Panzer divisions, so essential for counter-attack, were no longer more than a shadow of what they had been. The consequences of an insufficient inspection and test programme at the end of the factory assembly-lines were mechanical defects which became more and more frequent in the new machines reaching the front. So the number of tanks available to each division daily was no more than five or six.

Even though it is true that the losses of the 2nd Ukrainian Front since October 6 had not been light, it still maintained an enormous numerical and *matériel* advantage over its adversary.

Faced with this situation, Hitler agreed to send three new Panzer divisions into Hungary. These were the 3rd, 6th, and 8th Panzer Divisions. He also sent three battalions of Panther tanks. But while waiting for these reinforcements to be put into line, Army Group "South" had to fall back from the Tisza above Tokay and dig in on the heights of the Mátra mountains, overlooking Hatvan, Eger, and Miskolc. It had to limit its counter-attacks to local actions only, as a result of the previously mentioned exhaustion of its men and equipment. And so the curtain fell on the third act of this tragedy, the overall direction of which was assumed by Marshal Timoshenko in the name of the *Stavka*.

6th Army forced back by Tolbukhin

The curtain rose again on November 27 with the appearance on the stage of the forces of the 3rd Ukrainian Front, available now that Belgrade had surrendered. On that day, Marshal Tolbukhin unexpectedly forced the Danube at Mohacs. This was 125 miles up river from Belgrade past the confluence of the Drava and the Danube. Brushing aside the weak defences of the 2nd *Panzerarmee,* his 57th Army swept along a line from Pécs to Kaposvár and, by December 5, called a halt after an advance of 75 miles between the south-west tip of Lake Balaton and the River Drava at Barcs.

On December 3, on Tolbukhin's right, the 3rd Guards Army arrived at Dunaföldvár, 60 miles north of Mohacs. As a result, in order to avoid its right being rolled up, the German 6th Army could only pull back along a line Lake Balaton– Lake Velencei–Budapest.

Tolbukhin's advance northward allowed his partner Malinovsky to re-arrange his deployment yet again. At the

foot of the Mátra mountains, he built up a strategic battering-ram, with the Pliev Group and the 6th Guards Tank Army. Near Hatvan on December 7, the exhausted German 6th Army broke under the force of the attack launched by the Russians and, several days later, Pliev reached the elbow formed by the Danube above the Hungarian capital and could now bring the strings of barges which supplied it under the fire of his artillery. Furthermore, between the Danube and the Mátra mountains, on December 14, Soviet armour captured Ypolisag. And so the Russians had almost completely outflanked the right of the 8th Army, and were once more threatening to hem it in against the Carpathians.

Last desperate effort

However the 8th Panzer Division, newly arrived, was immediately put under the command of LVII Panzer Corps, and this formation kept disaster at bay. Friessner would have liked to reinforce Kirchner with the 3rd and the 6th Panzer Divisions, which had just been stationed on the isthmus which separates Lakes Balaton and Velencei. If they hurried, he maintained, there was a great opportunity to crush the 6th Guards Tank Army, which was in a salient around Ypolisag. When Hitler received this proposal, he ordered Friessner to attack from the isthmus between the two lakes and to throw Tolbukhin back to the Danube. To which the commander of Army Group "South" retorted that the state of the ground between Lake Balaton and the Danube, after long weeks of sleet and rain, was absolutely impassable.

Wrong compromise

Guderian forced a very poor compromise in this dispute on December 18: the *Führerbefehl* would be carried out when frost had hardened the ground. Meanwhile, the 3rd and 6th Panzer Divisions would cross the Danube at Komarom, carry out Friessner's proposed counter-attack, but leave their tank battalions behind. In vain did Friessner protest that this plan would deprive them of their entire striking power. He was told that he should either obey or resign.

△ △ △ *The pale light of dawn: the Hun surveys the empty seats of the Axis defaulters.*
△ △ *Stalin's lengthening shadow in the south, from the* London *Punch.*
△ *A "family scene in Central Europe", from the* London Star. *"It's nothing, mother," says Hungary. "I'm opening a second front with Rumania."*

The German *Mittlerer Zugkraftwagen* 8t SdKfz 7 half-track carrier

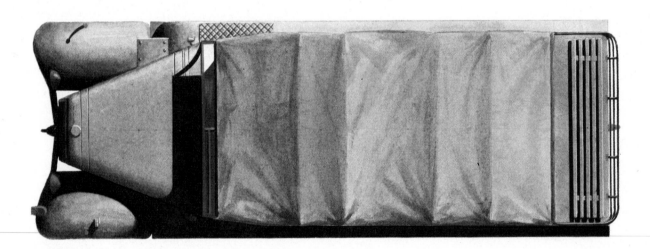

Weight: 11.5 tons.
Crew: 12.
Engine: one Maybach HL 62 TUK inline, 140-hp.
Speed: 31 mph.
Range: 250 miles.
Length: 20 feet 3 inches.
Width: 7 feet 10½ inches.
Height: 8 feet 7 inches.

Tolbukhin's advantage

Forty-eight hours later, Tolbukhin was attacking the sector between the Danube and Lake Balaton defended by III Panzer and LXXII Corps (General August Schmidt) of the 6th Army. In front of him roved a first echelon of about ten divisions which, very cleverly, moved along the roads impassable to tanks because of the soft terrain. Between the river and Lake Velencei, the 217th *Volksgrenadier* Division was crushed on the first day. Between Lake Velencei and Lake Balaton, the 153rd Infantry Division and the 1st and 23rd Panzer Divisions defended the little mediaeval town of Székesfehérvár to the end, without the tanks held in reserve by Guderian's express order being of any help to them. By December 24, all was over and the Kremlin communiqué claimed that the Germans had lost 12,000 dead, 5,468 prisoners, 311 tanks, and 248 guns destroyed or captured.

On the same day Tolbukhin launched his armoured formations through this gap, now over 40 miles wide. On December 27, after an excursion of 55 miles through the rearguard of the Army Group "South", they occupied Esztergom on the right bank of the Danube and, from the other side of the river, recognised the 6th Guards Tank Army that LVII Panzer Corps had been quite unable to dislodge.

Budapest besieged

On December 1, the Führer had proclaimed that the Hungarian capital was a "fortress". This took it out of the authority of Army Group "South". The garrison consisted of the S.S. IX Mountain Corps (General Pfeffer-Wildenbruch). When Friessner realised that the 3rd Ukrainian Front was attacking, he wanted to take it in flank by a counter-attack with this corps, but the manoeuvre would involve the evacuation of Budapest. So, on the night of December 22/23, Friessner was relieved and ordered to hand over to General Wöhler. Fretter-Pico shared his disgrace.

Two S.S. cavalry divisions, the 13th

△ *A scene typical of the street fighting in which the Russians took Budapest street by street, house by house, reducing it virtually to rubble in the process. Note the "dragon's teeth" anti-tank obstacles in the background.*

This is the version that Friessner gives of this episode, and Guderian's silence on it seems to indicate that he agrees.

Panzer Division, and the *"Feldherrnhalle" Panzergrenadier* Division were thus caught in the trap. Having got them cut off, Hitler now had to get them out, so without consulting O.K.H., he robbed Army Group "Centre", which was responsible for the defence of East Prussia. He took IV S.S. Panzer Corps (General Gille: 3rd *"Totenkopf"* Panzer Division and 5th *"Wiking"* Panzer Division) and sent them over the Carpathians. This order was made on Christmas Day, and, though Guderian tried to have the units recalled, he wrote:

"All my protests were useless. Hitler thought it was more important to free the city of Budapest than to defend Eastern Germany."

All the same, Hitler was acting more logically than Guderian gives him credit for. The day before, while Guderian tried to draw Hitler's attention to the increasing number of signs pointing to a coming Soviet offensive between the Carpathians and the Niemen, the Führer had riposted:

"Now, my dear General, I do not believe in this Russian attack. It is all a gigantic bluff. The figures produced by your 'Foreign Armies: East' section are far too exaggerated. You worry too much. I am firmly convinced that nothing will happen in the East."

Obsession with the Soviet threat could deceive Major-General Gehlen, head of "Foreign Armies: East" of O.K.H.; it could even impress Colonel-General Guderian. But it had no effect on the far-sightedness and *sang froid* of the Führer!

RUSSIA'S WAR EFFORT

1. *After an evacuation of plant, still not fully comprehended in the Western world, at the beginning of the war, the Russians started afresh behind the Urals, and by the last year of the war were turning out huge quantities of basic, but perfectly adequate, weapons, such as the 76.2-mm guns seen here. This weapon was the standard divisional ordnance.*
2. *Soviet might advances to victory, which was won, at great cost, by the effective combined action of infantry, armour, and ground-attack aircraft.*

Soviet Russia was the country which made the biggest land contribution to the Allied cause in World War II—an obvious fact which is often overlooked. By 1945 the Red Army's total strength—deployed on all fronts from Siberia and Manchuria to Persia and Europe—amounted to some 500 divisions. To equip and supply this immense host was a superb achievement, rendered even more impressive by the fact that the bulk of the work had been accomplished in the "crisis year" of 1941-42.

Draconian measures had been measures to evacuate as much industrial material as possible to the east—but draconian measures alone could never have achieved such fantastic results without the wholesale co-operation of the Soviet workers. This was,

quite simply, the biggest integration of the civilian population with national war effort in the whole of World War II. Reams of figures have been quoted with justifiable pride by Soviet historians. The following are a few examples.

All records were broken when it came to setting up new blast furnaces in the Urals and getting them into operation. Before the war it had taken two and a half years to build a new blast furnace. But at the great war production centre at Magnitogorsk in the Urals two new furnaces were set up in eight months, a time sliced to seven months at Chusovaya. Whisked lock, stock, and barrel from Zaporozh'ye on the Dniepr, the Engels plant was going full blast a mere 20 days after arriving at its new site.

And at Moscow the military plan of the Armaments Commissaria was loaded *en masse* on to 1 trains in the middle of Octobe 1941—the month when the capita was declared to be in a state o siege—travelled east for 11 days and was in production by the end of the first week in December—with an output 50 per cen higher than it had been befor the evacuation.

Bear in mind that these feat were achieved in the Russia winter, on completely new site as often as not, where the worker had to build their own camp in temperatures of –40 degrees C With a new mass call-up for th Red Army, this necessitated complete overhaul of the Sovie labour force. In 1942 alon 4,400,000 workers were eithe trained or "re-educated", an

ПО ВРАЖЬЕЙ ЗЕМЛЕ,
ВПЕРЕД К ПОБЕДЕ!

3

4

the number of women workers rose dramatically. And this was for heavy work. Women driving steam-engines rose in number from six per cent at the beginning of 1941 to 33 per cent by the end of 1942. For women operating forging and press machines the increase was from 11 per cent to 50 per cent, and for compressors the numbers rose from 27 per cent to 44 per cent.

In the 12 months between July 1941 and July 1942, 15,198 tanks were produced in the Soviet Union, helping to explain the Red Army's crushing "comeback" under Zhukov in the Stalingrad counter-offensive. The same applied to the aircraft industry – in particular to the mass production of the superb Il-2 "Shturmovik" – and to artillery. This did not merely apply to field artillery but to "infantry artillery" – mortars. Here again the initial German superiority was soon dwarfed by Soviet mass production.

Standardisation and mass production, it must be emphasised, were not the whole answer. It was an immense national effort, with civilian defence funds and collective farms clubbing together to buy "their" tanks for the army, much as happened in Britain and America. None of the figures or statistics can paint the full picture of the human side of this phenomenon, which had no parallel in world history down to 1945 and has only been matched since the end of World War II by the efforts of Communist China.

3. *Food for Russia's god of war. Major Soviet offensives were normally heralded by artillery barrages that rendered World War I barrages pale in comparison, and these consumed enormous quantities of ammunition. This photograph was taken in a Urals factory in 1943.*

4. *A T-34/76 tank assembly line in Leningrad. After standardising a simple but sound design, the Russians were able to turn out quantities of this vehicle that German tank production just could not hope to match.*

5. *A Russian shell factory. Visible is ammunition for light field artillery, ranging up to some for super-heavy guns.*

THE RUSSIAN PARTISANS

Despite the splendid reaction of the Soviet people during the months of the German advance into Russia, it was a profound embarrassment to Stalin's régime that the people in the German-occupied regions did not instantly rise in furious rebellion against their alien overlords. There were three clear reasons for this. The first was a genuine sense of bitterness at the speed at which the Red Army had been forced back to the east. There had been far too many scenes of Party officials heading the rush to get back eastwards on "essential" missions—resentment, in short, of the indecent "skedaddle" put up by officials and defenders of the régime. The second was the deceptive but understandable viewpoint that such a complete collapse must mean the defeat of the country; a canny sense of wait-and-see made itself felt. Third and most important was the fact that the Stanlinist régime had made no provision whatsoever for emergency resistance measures in the event of the western provinces becoming overrun by enemy forces. Stalin had proclaimed the Soviet people to be "monolithically united", and that was that.

The first step was taken on June 29, 1941, by the Central Committee of the Communist Party (one week after the invasion). This was a directive stating the need for partisan and sabotage activity in the west, and it was amplified by a radio speech by Stalin on July 3. This boiled down to an appeal to the people of Russia "to create unbearable conditions in the occupied areas for the enemy and all who help him, to pursue and destroy them at every step, to disrupt everything they do." But another fortnight of unmitigated disaster went by before the Party issued its first detailed directive on how such partisan activity was to be organised, with at least one resistance unit operating in every former Soviet administrative area. But this did not happen in the chaotic months of the late summer and autumn of 1941. It did not begin to materialise until much later. And in many areas it does not seem to have materialised at all.

To start with, it was obvious that initial partisan activity must be localised to areas where the terrain offered the best opportunities for survival—the Pripet marshes, the forests of Belorussia. In addition, weapons must be supplied or captured in sufficient quantity before any effective activity could begin. As the campaign of 1941 moved to its crisis and turning-point before Moscow, it is clear that the war of the partisans behind the German front line was the least of the Soviet régime's worries.

So for these reasons the Russian partisan war was conducted in a very low key in 1941. Certainly there was no tight Party control; and operations were led by officers cut off by the initial rout who decided to carry on by themselves with what they had—a handful of rifles and hand grenades and local volunteers who felt the same way. Certainly it was not until Zhukov's Moscow counter-offensive that there was any indication that the Soviet Union had a chance of survival, let alone of winning the war. And the Moscow battle saw the first real signs that partisans and regular Red Army forces could work together. In the Moscow–Tula–Kalinin area there were about 10,000 partisans, and although many of these had been sent behind the enemy lines—rather than having operated there from the start of the offensive—they certainly made their presence

1. *Partisans return to their hideout after an operation near Pinsk in 1944. Earlier in the war the wounded man might have been shot and left behind, but by 1944 the Belorussian partisans were well equipped even with medical facilities.*
2. *Partisans are sworn in to the Red Army. With thousands of able bodied and willing men and women cut off from the west of Russia by the German advance in 1941, great partisan bands were not difficult to raise. Supplied from the air, these bands tied down considerable Germans forces on not very effective security duties and aided Russia's cause by cutting German communications.*

Объявление!

За пойманного бандита „КАТЮ" Германское Командование вознаградит поймавшего : 10 марок; 5 пудов соли, а также чным наделом в 25 гектар

felt during the Moscow offensive. Soviet records credit partisan activities during the *whole* of the winter of 1941-42 with having accounted for 18,000 Germans—well over the equivalent of a division. The sources for such statistics remain inscrutable. What is certain is that the Moscow battle saw the first German executions of prominent "partisan terrorist leaders"—Gurianov and Solntsev.

Not until May 30, 1942, did the Soviet High Command (*Stavka*) push through the establishment of a "Central Staff of the Partisan Movement". By this time recruitment was steadily increasing, largely due to the fact that the Germans had already revealed what their policy was going to be like in the occupied territories: brutal in the extreme. Still, any form of central supply system from Moscow remained basic; and it was not until the next crisis, that of September/October 1942, that the partisan "War of the Rails" (officially declared in July of the following year) began to make itself felt. It was instrumental in slowing up the Manstein-Hoth offensive which vainly tried to break through the ring of steel encircling the trapped 6th Army in Stalingrad.

As in so many other different ways, Stalingrad had an immense effect on the partisan movement. Its boost of Russian national morale coincided with an increased flow of armaments from Moscow—more food supplies, rifles and sub-machine guns, mortars, anti-tank guns for use on trains—even some heavy artillery —and medical supplies, which in many ways were the most important item of the lot as far as partisan morale was concerned. Soviet figures for Belorussia in 1943 assess the increase in the partisans' numbers as rising from 65,000 in February to 360,000 in December; for the Ukraine at the end of the year, 220,000.

In July 1943 the Soviet High Command gave its formal order for the launching of the "War of Rails"—the partisan "offensive" aimed at paralysing the German lines of supply. The immediate target was the German Army Group "Centre", which had to cope with the partisans in the Gomel, Orel, and Bryansk regions. Between July and the end of September over 17,000 rails had been blown by the partisans of the three regions, working in co-ordination. Matters were made even worse for the Germans

3. One of the most celebrated Russian partisans was a woman known as "Katya". In their efforts to catch her, the Germans offered several hundred marks, 180 pounds of salt, and about 62 acres of land for any Russian who would turn her in, as in this poster sent out by the district Kommandantur of Dobrush in Belorussia.
4. Smolensk partisans, all well armed with PPSh sub-machine guns.
5. Not so well equipped: Donbass partisans in 1942, with a motley assortment of captured and indigenous weapons.
6. The Smolensk area again. Men of the "Kletnyanskaya" Brigade on parade. By 1944 many of the larger partisan units were in effect proper army formations, lacking only the uniform to complete the transformation.

in Belorussia, where between **7**
August and November 200,000
rails were blown, 1,014 trains
wrecked or derailed, and 72 railway bridges destroyed or badly
damaged. The effect on the German railway net was impressive:
two-thirds of the Belorussian lines
were effectively put out of action
for weeks at a time, and for the
space of ten days the key Minsk-
Molodechno line was blocked.

Some of the accounts of the
partisan war lay excessive stress
on its daredevil side–raiding a
German H.Q. at Christmas and
shattering the Teutonic festivi-
ties with hand grenades, or the
gruesome fate of High Com-
missioner Wilhelm Kube of Belorussia, blown to eternity by
a time-bomb put under his bed
by his (partisan) Belorussian girl
friend. But in reality the partisan
war served as much to increase
Russia's agony as to speed the
day of the Germans' departure.
German reprisals were heavy-
handed and ruthless, with whole
villages being wiped out, Lidice-
style. As German atrocities were
always one of the most compelling
sources of partisan recruitment
this created a vicious circle which
only added to the tragedy.

When the great Red Army advances began, with their paths
paved by partisan operations,
the partisans found that their
war was not over: they were
drafted into the Red Army.

Although slow to get under
way, Russia's partisan movement
grew apace. At its height at least
half a million patriots fought
in the partisan ranks.

7. *In Odessa, the partisans hid in the city's catacombs, from one of which they are here seen emerging.*

8. *A partisan column in southern Russia. Further to the north the partisans had forests and marshes in which to hide, and further to the south mountains, but in the plains, mobility was of the essence in evading the Germans.*

9. *By 1943 many of Russia's provinces were largely in the hands of the partisans, and here they could operate as ordinary troops, as this photograph of partisans in the Pinsk area indicates. Note the DP light machine gun providing covering fire.*
Overleaf: *Russian cavalry charge.*

'For the Motherland, for Stalin!'

10

11

12

Although by 1945 the Red Army, the biggest in the world, could field the greatest concentration of armoured power in the world, it was basically as it had been for centuries: an infantry force. Its masses of "foot-sloggers", plain and simple, were in the long run the basic factor which ground down the resistance of the Wehrmacht.

Four nine-men sections made up a platoon; three platoons, plus a mortar platoon, a machine gun section, and a medical section made up a company. Three companies made up a battalion, which also had a machine gun company, a mortar company, an anti-tank platoon, an anti-tank troop (the platoon being armed with anti-tank rifles and the troop with two 57-mm guns), a medical platoon, and a supply platoon. And

three battalions made up the normal rifle regiment (about 2,500 men, under a colonel or lieutenant-colonel), which was the smallest numbered formation in the Red Army.

Then came the rifle division of three rifle regiments, plus supply, veterinary, and medical services, a divisional staff, an artillery regiment, an anti-tank battalion, an anti-tank rifle company, an A.A. artillery company, and both engineer and signals battalions. Two to four divisions made up a corps; two to four corps made up an army, and anything from three to 14 armies made up a "front" or army group.

In addition to the basic, all-arms army there were the guards armies. "Guards" was an honorific title given to any unit down to regiment which had especially

distinguished itself in action. Then there was the "shock" army, a special formation made up of experienced units, plus more fire-power and artillery, for particularly formidable attacks; and the "tank" army.

In attack the massed Soviet infantry was given lavish artillery, armoured, and air support; but the outcome of the assault inevitably depended on the infantry. Soviet tactics – even those of ace commanders such as Zhukov, Konev, and Rokossovsky – tended to be basic. Eisenhower, in his memoirs, recalls how he met Zhukov after the war and asked him the secret of the Red Army's massive breakthroughs and advances. The Allied Supreme Commander was horrified when Zhukov obliged. Reminding Eisenhower of the faith

10. *In the north, the Russians had learned the lessons of the Winter War against Finland well. Now they had properly trained ski troops and specialised equipment, such as the sledge seen here, for moving supplies and weapons that could not be carried by men. The machine gun is a 7.62-mm SPM, which weighed fractionally under 100 pounds.*
11. *Front line medical aid: Nurse Liza Kozyukova in northern Russia.*
12. *Cold is not the prerogative only of northern Russia, as can be seen in this photograph of a Russian attack in the Ukraine, which can be (and often was in World War II) as cold as areas many hundreds of miles further north.*

13. *More specialised equipment: tank-towed sledges for troops and supplies. In this photograph, Russian ski troops are getting an easy ride up to the front.*

the Germans pitted in extensive minefields, Zhukov said that the Russian way was to send the first wave in *without lifting the mines.* They suffered murderous casualties, it was true, but the second wave had a much easier time. And the third wave . . .

But it is unwise to draw generalisations from this. Soviet tactics varied considerably. One trick used in the attacks on the Baltic front was to plaster the German lines with shellfire but leave regular gaps along the line. While the Germans were still being bombarded and keeping their heads down, the Soviet attack would be launched up the "corridors" between their own shells into these gaps. Given any major inaccuracy in the fire-plan the Soviet infantrymen in the attack were bound to suffer badly from their own shells. But by the time the bombardment lifted and the Germans prepared for an orthodox defence, they would find the Russians as far as a mile behind them already.

Inexhaustible reinforcements of men and machines lay at the disposal of the Soviet commanders and they were never loath to make

full use of them. But by 1945 there were new trends emerging from the traditional, heads-down tactics which had bulldozed the Wehrmacht from the Volga to the gates of Berlin. For a start, the Red Army was becoming mobile. This was largely due to the Western Allies. The tanks they sent to Russia may not have measured up to the gruelling standards of the Eastern Front, but the transport was another matter. By the end of the war Russia had been sent 427,000 trucks, over 2,000 Ordnance vehicles, and 35,000 motor-cycles, and over two million tyres. For the first time in its history the Red Army had been "put on wheels", and began to get the fullest benefit out of the deadly advantages of modern mobile warfare.

This came to full fruition in the very last campaign which the Soviet Union fought in World War II: the attack on the Japanese Kwantung Army in Manchuria. This was an extremely sophisticated affair, using all arms: Army, Air Force, and Marines. Mass parachute drops speeded the advance, which was carried

out with close co-ordination between the various units.

The wheel had indeed come full circle from the first, frantic battles of 1941, when the long brown ranks, arms linked, had charged the German machine guns with roars of *"Urra!"* until the sickened German gunners could hardly bring themselves to keep firing. But even in these disastrous days the Russian soldier had shown his best quality: incredible endurance. This was typified by the almost-forgotten siege of Brest-Litovsk, right on the start-line of "Barbarossa", which held out for an incredible month until July 24.

This was the spirit of Stalingrad, which the Western Allies were proud to honour. By the end of 1941 the Red Army had saved its country from annihilation. By the end of 1942 it had proved itself a match for the Wehrmacht, and that the Soviet Union might well beat Germany without Allied aid, given time. And by the end of 1943 it had gained the initiative, never to lose it, and proved itself the greatest Allied instrument of victory.

CHAPTER 136
Eisenhower slows down

On the eve of the German offensive in the Ardennes it was possible to discern on the Allied side a certain degree of frustration similar to that prevailing in Britain and America immediately before the break-through at Avranches.

On September 15, victory seemed to be close at hand. Three months later, General Eisenhower could indeed claim to have liberated Mulhouse, Belfort, Strasbourg, and Metz, to have taken Aix-la-Chapelle (Aachen), cleared Antwerp and the Scheldt estuary, and taken more than 150,000 prisoners. Nevertheless, on December 15 the Rhine bridges and Ruhr basin were, if anything, further away from the Allied armies than at the end of the summer. It was clear to everyone that between the present positions and the final objective, there would be more major battles; however, no one suspected that the first would be a defensive one.

The slowing down of the Allied thrust can be explained by a combination of factors: the weather, the terrain, the degrees of determination shown and decisions made by commanders on both sides of a front line that ran from the Swiss frontier to the North Sea. As far as the weather was concerned, persistent rain fell throughout the latter part of the summer and the autumn of 1944, so much so that during the Ardennes offensive Patton required his chaplain to write a prayer for fine weather. The unseasonable climate and the shorter days resulted in a disastrous drop in the number of sorties effected by the tactical air forces in support of the infantry. The figures below relating to the American 3rd Army are typical of the whole front:

August	12,292 missions	(396 per day)
September	7,791 missions	(260 per day)
October	4,790 missions	(154 per day)
November	3,509 missions	(117 per day)
December (1–22)	2,563 missions	(116 per day)

Knowing the use made of their "flying artillery" by the Allies in the battle of Normandy, it is not surprising that such a reduction told heavily on the Allied advance. Furthermore, the terrain was

▽ *Eisenhower, already short of men and supplies, was now further slowed in developing his broad-front offensive towards Germany by the torrential rain and resultant mud that characterised the autumn of 1944.*

now one of forest and mountain, country well-suited to a defensive strategy, in the sense that lines of attack were pressed into comparatively few axes that were easy to block. The Vosges, Hunsrück, and Eifel were such regions, and, in addition, their vast forests made aerial reconnaissance virtually impossible and reduced considerably the feasibility of air support. On the plains of Lorraine, the defence made good use of flooded rivers as natural obstacles, as well as of the system of fortifications round Metz and Thionville. The Rur and the *Westwall* system fulfilled the same rôle in the Aix-la-Chapelle (Aachen) sector.

The British and Canadians soon found themselves obliged to mount amphibious operations.

Manpower shortages

As regards strategic factors behind the hold-up, it should be remarked that in Washington General Marshall had been somewhat over-stringent in calculating the numbers to allocate to American ground forces, and that Eisenhower now found himself short of divisions, although it had seemed improbable that after two months of movement and retreat the enemy would manage to establish himself on a continuous front of some 500 miles,

and thwart some 60 Allied divisions in their hopes of achieving a decisive breakthrough. In these circumstances, the Pentagon was obliged to turn various anti-aircraft units into infantry units, but the inactivity of the Luftwaffe caused no problem here.

Even so, at the time of transferring S.H.A.E.F. from Granville to Versailles, Eisenhower would have been somewhat embarrassed if a miracle had brought him the 30 additional divisions he needed to return to the attack. As it was, the logistic problem of keeping 60 divisions in the field was being dealt with in a way that caused considerable dissatisfaction among those at the front.

Divergent aims

The capture of Antwerp enabled Allied strategy to end the vicious circle, although it took Field-Marshal Montgomery one month and reinforcement by two American divisions to achieve this; and during the delay two divergent operations, in flagrant disregard of the "concerted thrust" which Montgomery had urged, took place. While the British 2nd Army, its right flank at Grave on the Maas, its left at Eindhoven, mounted an attack north-west towards Tilburg and Breda, the American 1st and 9th Armies

▽ *Japanese American infantry of the 2nd Battalion, 442nd Combat Team, move up a muddy French road towards their bivouac area. At the beginning of the war American Japanese were distrusted by the government and most of the population of the United States, but later on, Japanese units serving in the European theatre proved to be loyal and efficient combat troops.*

were trying to breach the *Westwall* in the Aix-la-Chapelle (Aachen) sector, with the aim of reaching the Rhine below Cologne.

Obviously, Eisenhower's task was not an easy one. To appease Patton, he organised an American 9th Army on September under the command of Lieutenant-General William H. Simpson, with the immediate objective of taking Brest. Once this fortress had fallen, the 9th Army was shifted to the Ardennes front, then on October 23, to the left of the 1st Army, with which it participated in the November offensive on the *Westwall*. Coming under General Bradley's command, it provided the linchpin with the British and Canadian 21st Army Group.

On September 15, at Vittel, Lieutenant-General Jacob L. Devers assumed command of a new Allied 6th Army Group, directly subordinate to S.H.A.E.F. and responsible for the conduct of operations between Epinal and the Swiss frontier. In the course of these changes, Army Detachment "B" was designated as French 1st Army on September 19. Then, to give Generals Patch and de Lattre homogeneous sectors, the French II and American VI Corps were interchanged. On September 29 General Patton was ordered to hand his XV Corps over to the American 7th Army.

Such was the disposition of the Allied armies in preparation for the autumn campaign.

The German forces

On September 4, when Hitler relieved Field-Marshal von Rundstedt as Commander-in-Chief in the West, a document prepared at O.K.W. gave the following situation for the German Army on the Western Front.

	Infantry divisions	Panzer divisions
Completely fit	13	3 (+ 2 brigades)
Partially fit	12	2 (+ 2 brigades)
Totally unfit	14	7
Dissolved	7	–
In process of reorganisation	9	2

Hence Rundstedt was faced with the task of giving battle with 30 divisions (five of them Panzer), these to be joined by 11 divisions being reorganised, thus enabling those qualified as "totally unfit" to be pulled back. Furthermore, Hitler intended to despatch 28 further divisions to the West, these being 28 of the 43 "people's grenadier divisions" (*Volksgrenadierdivisionen*), which Himmler, as commander of the reserves, was hastily preparing for the line. Their standard of training was very poor, their complement was on the small side (10,000 to 12,000), and their equipment was inferior.

Lieutenant-General William "Big Bill" Simpson graduated from the same class at West Point Military Academy as Patton and Hodges in 1909. The three officers served together in World War I and remained life-long friends. Simpson took over command of the 9th Army on September 5, 1944 and led the army in the American counter-offensive after the Ardennes. 9th Army's assault over the Rur was the last American set-piece assault in Europe. Eisenhower described Simpson as a man "who never made a mistake".

The German *Panzerjäger* Panther or *Jagdpanther* tank destroyer

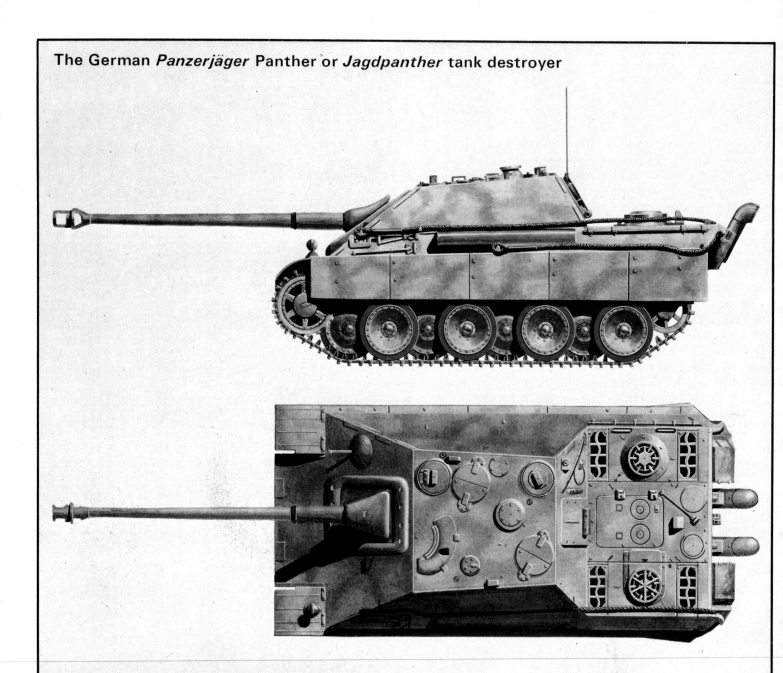

Weight: 46 tons.
Crew: 5.
Armament: one 8.8-cm PaK 43/3 gun with 60 rounds and one 7.92-mm MG 34 machine gun with 600 rounds.
Armour: hull nose 60-mm, front plate 80-mm, upper sides 50-mm, lower sides, hull rear, and superstructure 40-mm, decking 17-mm, belly 15-mm, and mantlet 120-mm.
Engine: one Maybach HL 230 P30 inline, 700-hp.
Speed: 28 mph on roads, 15 mph cross-country.
Range: 100 miles on roads, 50 miles cross-country.
Length: 33 feet 3 inches.
Width: 10 feet 10 inches.
Height: 8 feet 11 inches.

In addition, three more Panzer brigades were assigned to Rundstedt, each of them comprising a battalion of 68 Panthers. At the same time, ten assault gun brigades, several *Nebelwerfer* brigades, and ten battalions of anti-tank vehicles, some of them equipped with the new and devastating *"Jagdpanther"*, were sent to him. By sacrificing the fully traversing turret, this vehicle combined in its 46 tons the speed of a Panther with the fire-power of a *"Königstiger"*, with an 8.8-cm, 71-calibre gun.

In fact, there was no shortage of new *matériel* in the arsenals of the Third Reich. While it was perfectly true that, at the front, Army Group "B" could only muster 100 operational tanks, factory production during the summer, in spite of air raids, totalled 1,500. At Dompaire, on September 16, it was estab-lished that some of the tanks belonging to the 112th Panzer Brigade, demolished by the French 2nd Armoured Division, bore the manufacturing date of August 15. At Friesen on November 23, *Jagd-panthers* which were roughly handled by the French 5th Armoured Division during General de Lattre's offensive in upper Alsace, had left Nuremberg only 12 days previously.

Rundstedt's objective

"I must hold on for six weeks," Rund-stedt wrote on September 7, 1944 in his first report to O.K.W. But if fortune denied General Weygand the 11-day res-pite he sought on June 4, 1940, a pause in the fighting of 65 days was granted to

△ *Sherman tank crews of the American 3rd Armoured Division wait at the edge of a forest for their attack to begin. Allied tanks were completely outclassed by such German vehicles as the* Jagdpanther, *their only advantage being the extra manoeuvrability bestowed on them by powerful engines and low weight.*

"I insist upon the importance of Antwerp... I am prepared to give you everything for the capture of the approaches to Antwerp"

Eisenhower

Walcheren in 1944 was to the British an ill-starred place: in 1809 a landing on the island had met with total disaster, and now in the autumn of World War II it was the final obstacle to the opening of the Scheldt estuary and the port of Antwerp. The Allies had cleared the rest of the estuary, and advanced the 157th Brigade as far as the causeway linking Zuid-Beveland with Walcheren. But the defences of the island, entrusted to the 70th Division, looked formidable, with some 50 7.5- to 22-cm guns and nearly 10,000 men. Rather than launch a frontal attack, 21st Army Group decided that bombers should blow breaches in the sea walls to flood the centre of the island, and then the 155th Brigade should cross from Bres-

kens to land in Flushing while the 4th Special Service Brigade made a landing at Westkapelle.

The operation proved difficult but straightforward. Bombers blew open two breaches in the sea defences on the south-west side of the island and one each on the north-east and south-east sides, flooding most of the interior of the island with the exception of the town of Middelburg. The landings went in with heavy gun-fire and air support at about dawn, and soon took Westkapelle and Flushing, the last resistance in the latter ending on November 4. Meanwhile the "rim" of the Walcheren "saucer" had been secured, and the Allies pushed on to Middelburg, where General Daser surrendered with his last 2,000 men on the 6th.

1. *Rescue for men from a landing craft sunk on the approach to Walcheren.*
2. *Walcheren: a dismal spot, but one of the keys to the port of Antwerp.*
3. *American patrol boats in the Scheldt estuary.*
4. *An American light tank is swayed ashore at Antwerp, a vast port just behind the Allied front line.*
5. *The Walcheren landings.*

▷ *French infantry advance with tank support through a forest in Alsace.*

▽ *A Polish Bren gunner prepares to give covering fire during the battle for Breda in Holland.*
▽▷ *Cromwell cruiser tanks of the Polish 1st Armoured Division move up past a Dutch windmill.*

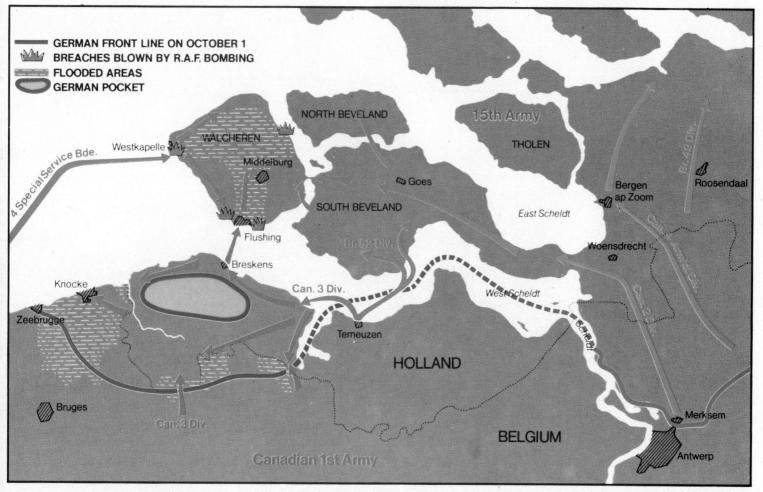

NORTH BEVELAND

15th Army

WALCHEREN

THOLEN

Westkapelle

Middelburg

Goes

Roosendaal

Bergen ap Zoom

4 Special Service Bde.

SOUTH BEVELAND

East Scheldt

Woensdrecht

Br. 52 Div.

Flushing

Breskens

West Scheldt

Br. 49 Div.

Can. 3 Div.

Knocke

Terneuzen

Zeebrugge

HOLLAND

Bruges

Can. 3 Div.

Merksem

BELGIUM

Antwerp

Canadian 1st Army

Rundstedt, General Bradley being unable to unleash his armies in the drive for the Saar and the Ruhr until November 8.

On October 1 or thereabouts, O.B.W. was responsible for 41 infantry divisions and ten Panzer or *Panzergrenadier* divisions. On November 26, according to O.K.W. records, these figures were 49 and 14 respectively. Even granted that most of these units were below strength, the effort implicit here in relation to the tricky situation of September 6 was remarkable.

After Arnhem, Rundstedt had two army groups under his command:

1. Army Group "B", in position between the estuary of the Scheldt to a point south of Trier (Treves), still under the command of Field-Marshal Model, Rundstedt's predecessor as Commander-in-Chief in the West.

Under Model's command were the 15th Army (General von Zangen), whose task was to prevent the enemy obtaining access to the Scheldt estuary; the 1st Parachute Army (Colonel-General Student), at the head of the Arnhem salient between the Tilburg and Venlo areas; and the 7th Army, blocking the way to Cologne,

△ An American Gun Motor
Carriage M12, a 155-mm "Long
Tom" gun on a Sherman
chassis, in action near the
Moselle. Note the crewman in the
foreground with his hands over
his ears to avoid concussion,
the firer at left holding the
lanyard in his right hand, the
gun at full recoil, and the
spade at the rear of the vehicle
dug into the ground to help take
up some of the recoil.
▷ An American Sherman
blasts a German strongpoint.

Koblenz and Trier, with, at its head, General Brandenberger, who had succeeded General Eberbach when the latter was taken prisoner at Amiens.

2. The area from south of Trier to the Swiss frontier was the responsibility of Army Group "G". On Hitler's orders, Colonel-General Blaskowitz had handed over command on September 22 to General Balck, whose record on the Russian front was a distinguished one. Army Group "G" consisted of the 1st Army, command of which had been assumed by General Schmidt von Knobelsdorff, who had made a name for himself at the head of XLVIII Panzer Corps, on September 6, with the task of blocking the route to Saarbrücken from a point north of Thionville to the Château Salins region; the 5th *Panzerarmee* (General von Manteuffel replacing the wounded General Hausser), blocking the way to Strasbourg from positions in front of the Vosges between Château Salins and Saint Dié; and the 19th Army (General Wiese) holding a position on the upper Moselle and defending the Belfort gap on the Doubs above Montbéliard.

Hitler's grandiose scheme

But the idea of a large-scale and decisive counter-offensive was already in the Führer's mind. As early as September 1, realising the Allies' logistic problems, he urged O.B.W. to hurl the 5th *Panzerarmee* from the Nancy–Neufchâteau area on

▽ *American self-propelled 155-mm guns start their barrage against the* Westwall. *Note that the front of each vehicle has been driven onto a ramp, to allow the guns a higher elevation and hence greater range.*

Rheims with a view to cutting the American 3rd Army's lines of communication. The scheme was a hopeless one and its failure brought about Blaskowitz's disgrace.

On September 19, Hitler's strategic reflections bore fruit again. He summoned General Balck, commander designate of Army Group "G", and Major-General von Mellenthin, his chief-of-staff, and, in Mellenthin's words, gave them the following appreciation of the situation: "According to the Führer, the British and American advance would come to a standstill on a line running from the mouths of the Scheldt, along the *Westwall* as far as Metz and from there along the Vosges. Supply problems would force the enemy to halt, and Hitler declared that he would make use of this pause to launch a counter-offensive in Belgium. He spoke of mid-November as the proper moment for such an operation."

The longer nights and late autumn mists would provide cover from Allied air reconnaissance and allow the plans to be prepared and carried out, and Hitler had taken the steps of ordering the formation of a 6th *Panzerarmee,* under the command of Colonel-General Sepp Dietrich of the *Waffen*-S.S., and of fetching the May 1940 *"Fall Gelb"* dossier from the archives.

On September 22, while the Battle of Arnhem was at its height, Eisenhower telegraphed Montgomery as follows (according to Colonel Stacey, official historian of the Canadian Army): ". . . I insist upon the importance of Antwerp. As I have told you I am prepared to give you everything for the capture of the approaches to Antwerp, including all the air forces and anything else you can support. Warm regard. Ike." The note of urgency detectable here would seem to suggest that Montgomery was so taken up with the vision of a lightning break-through towards Westphalia that he had come to give secondary consideration to Eisenhower's orders for the capture of Antwerp. However, failure at Arnhem made Montgomery more prepared to listen to Eisenhower, who this time offered him not only the air strength promised on September 22 but also the American 7th Armoured and 104th Divisions. But by the end of September, the German 15th Army, consisting of three corps (seven divisions), had had time to take up strong defensive positions and, even more important, recover morale, which had been badly shaken over the previous weeks. In the main, it responded to General von Zangen's appeal contained in an order of the day on October 7, where Antwerp was referred to as ". . . after Hamburg, the biggest port in Europe.

"When they have taken the Scheldt fortifications, the British will then be

◁ *The French town of Epinal has long been celebrated for its military prints, such as this one designed in 1945 by Hansi. It depicts the Allied alliance sweeping the Nazis out of Alsace-Lorraine.*

△ *The Allied advance continues: an American Sherman about to cross the Moselle by means of a pontoon bridge. With a few notable exceptions, such as Remagen, the Germans demolished all the bridges they left behind very efficiently. It is greatly to their credit that the Allied engineers managed to bridge the gaps thus left with great speed. It is worth noting, however, that the size and weight restrictions of the standard Allied bridges were to a certain extent responsible for the design of the small, light tanks that proved so inferior to their German counterparts.*

▷ An American bazooka team waits on the Dutch-German border for Panzer prey. The punch of the bazooka was so great that many German tank commanders who had had their vehicles knocked out by one of them thought they had been hit by a 6-inch shell.

▽ U.S. infantry advance into the suburbs of Metz.

able to unload enormous quantities of *matériel* in a large and perfectly protected harbour. With this *matériel* they could deal a deadly blow to the northern German plains and to Berlin before the onset of winter . . . The German people are watching us. At this moment the Scheldt fortifications play a crucial part in our future. Every day in which we can deny access to the port of Antwerp to the enemy and his resources could be vital."

The fighting that followed was thus very bitter. With General Crerar ill, Lieutenant-General Simonds led the Canadian 1st Army's attack. In the first phase, the British I Corps (Lieutenant-General Crocker) moved northwards from Antwerp, and on October 10 closed the Woensdrecht isthmus giving access to the island of Zuid-Beveland, but only with heavy losses. Meanwhile, the Canadian II Corps (Major-General Foulkes) set about cleaning up the bridgehead, where the Germans had been able to hold on, with the help of flooding, between Knocke and a point opposite Terneuzen. This took three weeks (October 6-26), even though two and subsequently three divisions were ranged against the single 64th Division. According to Major Shulman of Canadian Army Intelligence, the German division put up "an admirable piece of defensive fighting.

"Utilising their experience to the full, they took advantage of the flooded terrain in which they fought and forced the Canadians to rely on the narrow roads and dykes for their forward movement. The morale of the defenders heightened with each day they continued to resist, and General Eberding succeeded in instilling in his troops that will to fight which had been lacking in the Channel ports." Breskens, opposite Flushing (Vlissingen) fell on October 22, and on November 1 Eberding was taken prisoner.

On October 22, the left flank of the British 2nd Army (XII Corps) attacked from east to west towards 's-Hertogenbosch and Tilburg on a line converging with that taken by the Canadian right flank's thrust towards Breda. A second pincer movement from Woensdrecht and Terneuzen gave Zuid-Beveland to General Simonds on October 31. There remained Walcheren.

The centre of the island is below sea level and the breaching of the sea-dykes (effected with 1,263 tons of bombs) gave it the look of a saucer filled with water, with the defending troops clinging to the rim. These were men of the 70th Division (Lieutenant-General Daser), nicknamed the "White Bread Division", since it comprised men on a special diet for medical reasons. On November 1, with covering fire provided by the battleship *Warspite* and the monitors *Erebus* and *Roberts*, a brigade of Royal Marines landed at Westkapelle, while the British 52nd Division (Major-General E. Hakewill Smith) crossed the Scheldt between Breskens and Flushing. On November 3, resistance on the island was broken. Mopping up operations were completed on November 9, with the capture of Daser. In the meantime, Zangen, assisted by dreadful weather, had succeeded in putting the width of the lower Maas between his troops and the Canadian 1st Army.

It cost the Canadian 1st Army 12,873 killed, wounded, and missing to clear Antwerp, while itself taking 41,043 prisoners. From November 3 on, minesweepers went to work to clear the channel, and on the 28th the first convoy berthed in the great port, though on the previous day V-2's had claimed their first military and civil victims there.

But by then, two months had elapsed since the opportunity to take Antwerp on September 4 had occurred, and one is inclined to endorse Jacques Mordal's conclusion on the subject: "Allowing for 40,000 tons a day, the two months lost represented *matériel* amounting to 2,400,000 tons which, if supplied at the time required, would certainly have cost the Allies fewer disappointments in October. And possibly some might have been spared altogether if the people at S.H.A.E.F. had paid more heed to Admiral Ramsay, when he declared that he could think of nothing more vital than Operation 'Infatuate', the capture of Antwerp."

Struggle for the *Westwall*

The 12th Army Group was restricted operationally in October and November as a result of the continued serious shortage of fuel and munitions.

As we have seen, on the express instructions of Eisenhower, the American 3rd Army was especially hard hit in this

▽ *An American M10 tank destroyer in action in the streets of Aix-la-Chapelle. The M10 stemmed from the realisation early in the war that towed anti-tank guns would not be able to keep up with armoured formations, which nevertheless needed anti-tank protection. The 3-inch gun had a performance equal to that of the British 17-pounder and German 7.5-cm KwK 42, and was fitted in a new turret on the Sherman chassis. Production started in September 1942.*

△ *Lieutenant-General Courtney Hodges, whose 1st Army took Aix-la-Chapelle (Aachen)—the first city of the Third Reich to fall to the Western Allies.*

respect. And the 1st Army, to which General Bradley, acting on instructions, had given priority treatment, faced the *Westwall* and found itself attacking the Germans at their strongest points, since Hitler, Rundstedt, and Model were quite prepared to pay any price to block the principal route through to Cologne and the Ruhr.

So it was that the October battle for the *Westwall* took on the aspect of an "updated version of the Battle of the Somme" as foreseen by General Gamelin at the time of Munich. The attack was launched on October 8 on a five-mile front. Entrusted to the American XIX Corps (Major-General Corlett: 30th Infantry and 2nd Armoured Divisions), the attack was opened and supported by 372 105- to 240-mm guns and 396 twin-engined bombers and fighter-bombers, while 1,250 four-engined bombers operating on the edge of the sector pounded rail junctions and marshalling yards at Kassel, Hamm, and Cologne.

The attack proceeded slowly across the Wurm which, in the vicinity of Maastricht, constitutes the Dutch-German frontier. In five days, Corlett had advanced five miles across the German lines. However, this somewhat moderate success enabled General Hodges, commander of the 1st Army, to push his VII Corps (Major-General J. L. Collins) south-east, and by reaching Stolberg on October 10, to complete the encirclement of Aix-la-Chapelle, which had been started in September. The town, with its 4,000 defenders, was reduced by the 1st Division after a week's street fighting.

On the same date, the American 1st Army announced that it had taken 10,000 prisoners since D-Day. During the same period, it had fired more than 300,000 105- and 155-mm shells, but the munitions crisis now forced it to call a halt.

The 3rd Army, reduced to XII and XX Corps, was marking time in front of Metz. On the right, XII Corps advanced from the area of Grand Couronné to the Seille above and below Nomény; on the left, XX Corps had reached the Moselle between Metz and Thionville, but in the centre its repeated attempts to take *"Kronprinz"* fort, commanding the Nancy–Metz road at Ars-sur-Moselle, failed in spite of the use of napalm, flame-throwers, and machine guns. Detachments of the 5th Division which had found their way into its galleries were finally thrown back with heavy losses.

Montgomery or Bradley

On October 18, Eisenhower held a conference in Montgomery's headquarters in Brussels. The object of this meeting was to settle the strategic decisions which had to be taken before winter. No one favoured a defensive strategy, but there was disagreement between Montgomery, who urged a single thrust aimed at the Ruhr, and Bradley, who wanted a simultaneous thrust whereby the 3rd Army would be hurled at Mannheim and Frankfurt and the 9th at Cologne. In support of his thesis, Bradley put forward the arguments which he sums up as follows and which convinced Eisenhower:

"My reasoning on the *double* thrust was quite simple. Were Eisenhower to concentrate his November offensive

north of the Ardennes, the enemy could also concentrate his defences there the better to meet that single attack. On the other hand, if we were to split our effort into a double thrust with one pincer toward Frankfurt, we might both confound the enemy and make better use of the superior mobility of our Armies. Patton had the most at stake for if Montgomery's views were to prevail, Third Army would be consigned to the defensive south of the Ardennes and there perhaps wait out the war behind the Moselle River. Could not those divisions be better employed against the Saar, I asked S.H.A.E.F.?"

The northern attack got under way on November 16, and met only qualified success, although Generals Hodges (1st Army) and Simpson (9th Army) had engaged 14, and subsequently 17 divisions, including four armoured. On October 20, however, the 5th *Panzerarmee*

took up position between Brandenberger's right and Student's left. Consequently the defence gave ground, but held seven miles further back.

On December 10, a S.H.A.E.F. communiqué announced that between Düren and Linnich all resistance on the left bank of the Rur had stopped: this put the Americans within 25 miles of Cologne, but the communiqué failed to mention that the crossing of the Rur depended on a condition that had not been fulfilled. The American V Corps, attacking upstream, had not, in spite of repeated efforts, succeeded in taking the Rur and Erft dams. And, according to calculations made at General Bradley's headquarters, if the Germans were to breach these dams, an expanse of water, approximately $1\frac{1}{2}$ miles wide with a maximum depth of more than 25 feet, would form for a few days near Düren, effectively halting the Allied advance.

▽ *French M5 General Stuart light tanks during the liberation of Huningue on the Franco-Swiss frontier. The white cross on the water tower in the background indicates that it is in neutral Switzerland.*

CHAPTER 137
Into the Siegfried Line

▽ *U.S. infantry begin to move up into the* Westwall *or Siegfried Line, Germany's "impregnable" western border. The concrete obstacles were designed to halt tanks and the wire their accompanying infantry.*
▷ *American infantry take a walk along the serried rows of "dragons teeth" of the* Westwall.

Whilst Bradley's offensive in the north was at a standstill again, south of the Ardennes, Patton was preparing to force the *Westwall* in the region of Saarlouis, and had already chosen the date December 19 to do so. The transfer of the 5th *Panzerarmee* had left the defence of Lorraine to the German 1st Army alone. In spite of the addition of LXXXIX Corps (General Hoehn), this was reduced to nine divisions (each numbering on average fewer than 10,000 men) spread across a 125-mile front. Facing it, the American 3rd Army, reinforced to three corps (nine divisions, three of them armoured), numbered 250,000 men. Furthermore, Patton had the advantage of surprise, because, on November 8, the rain was so heavy that any important action seemed unlikely.

Sure enough, that evening, XII Corps (General M. S. Eddy: 26th, 35th, and 80th Infantry, 4th and 6th Armoured Divisions) threw aside the three feeble divisions which LXXXIX and XIII S.S. Corps (the latter under General Priess) put in its path and captured Moyenvic and Nomény. Eddy rapidly exploited this success: to the right along the line Château Salins – Morhange – Rohrbach (4th Armoured Division, 35th Infantry Division); to the left by Han-sur-Nied – Faulquemont – Saint Avold (6th Armoured Division, 80th Infantry Division) in spite of counter-attacks by the 17th S.S. *Panzergrenadier* Division *"Götz von Ber-*

Hanging out the washing - five years late

1. *The promise at last carried out: a member of the R.A.F. hangs out his washing on the Siegfried Line.*
2. *Anti-tank defences in the Siegfried Line.*
3. *Warrant Officer Millard Grary, an American of Scots extraction, practises the bagpipes amid the dragon's teeth of the Siegfried Line.*
4. *Last view of the vaunted Westwall for a group of German prisoners passing through it en route to a P.O.W. camp.*
5. *An innocent-looking barn disguises a concrete pillbox in the Westwall.*

lichingen", then by the 21st Panzer Division. Within XX Corps, the 5th Infantry Division set about outflanking Metz to the south and east of the fortress. The 95th Infantry Division (Major-General Twaddle) crossed the Moselle above Thionville during the night of November 8-9, then turning south met up with the 5th Infantry Division on November 19 on the Metz-Saarlouis road. This was the division's first experience under fire. Meanwhile, the 90th Infantry Division, which had forced a crossing of the Moselle below Thionville and which was followed by the 10th Armoured Division (Major-General W. H. H. Morriss), reached the Franco-German frontier on November 20.

Metz falls

The mopping up of Metz was entrusted to III Corps under Major-General J. Millikin. The fortress works mounted only 30 guns, and the 462nd *Volksgrenadier* Division which constituted its garrison numbered barely 7,000 men. On November 25, fighting in the centre of the town ceased and the Americans found Lieutenant-General Kittel, the fortress commander, severely wounded in hospital. The western fortifications fell one after the other. The "Jeanne d'Arc" Fort, which covered the district round Gravelotte, was the last to capitulate (December 13).

Patton into the *Westwall*

LXXXII Corps (General Sinnhuber) had no better success than XC and XIII S.S. Corps. Furthermore, the reserves which Army Group "G" and O.K.W. made available to give support to the 1st Army were in too poor shape to remedy the situation. So it was that Major-General Walker and his XX Corps were able to bite into the *Westwall*. On December 3, the 95th Infantry Division managed to secure by surprise the bridge over the Saar between Saarlouis and Fraulautern, on the right bank of the river, then secure the right bank area after reducing 50 pillboxes. On December 18, the 5th Infantry Division joined it in this bridgehead, while slightly downstream the 90th Infantry Division, overcoming two concrete positions, secured a second bridgehead occupying half of Dillingen.

2095

Patton's optimism with regard to the offensive he was preparing for December 19, with the help of 3,000 planes from the Tactical Air Force, appeared to be well grounded. Events would prove otherwise. Even so, between November 7 and December 21, at the cost of 4,530 dead, 21,300 wounded, and 3,725 missing, his army in Patton's own reckoning accounted for 21,300 Germans killed and 37,000 taken prisoner. At O.K.W. Hitler reacted to the 1st Army's defeat by dismissing General Schmidt von Knobelsdorff. On December 4 he was ordered to hand over his command to General Obstfelder.

Allied forces in Alsace reshuffled

If for the 12th Army Group victory on the Saar was to some extent compensation for failure on the Rur, the 6th Army Group won so convincing a victory in the Saverne gap and to the south of the Vosges that for a time it seemed likely it would reach positions along the left bank of the Rhine between Lauterbourg and Huningue. Fortunately for the Germans this did not occur, and the opportunity did not come about again.

It has been mentioned above that the American 7th Army had earlier been reinforced by XV Corps (79th Infantry Division and French 2nd Armoured Division). During October it also received the 44th, 100th, and 103rd Infantry Divisions, then after its breakthrough into lower Alsace, the 14th Armoured Division. And the French 1st Army, still responsible for the Mont Blanc–Barcelonnette sector, in addition to keeping its 2nd Moroccan Division (General Carpentier), received the 5th Armoured Division (General de Vernejoul), transferred from North Africa. At the end of November, the 4th Moroccan Mountain Division was relieved of its duties on the French-Italian border by the newly-constituted 27th (Alpine) Division and was transferred to the French 1st Army.

When he established his H.Q. at Vittel, General Devers had seven divisions under his command between Epinal and the Swiss frontier. At the start of the new offensive, his army group numbered 14 divisions, three of them armoured.

Outlining his new mission to him on September 19, Hitler had conveyed to

General Balck the paramount necessity, for political reasons, of holding Alsace and Lorraine at all costs. The transfer of the 5th *Panzerarmee* to the Rur sector was not compensated for, however, by new reinforcements, and the German 1st Army had to extend its left flank to block the way to Strasbourg between Château Salins and Raon-l'Etape. Meanwhile the 19th Army had taken up defensive positions on a line linking Saint Dié, Gérardmer, and the western spurs of the Vosges, and ending to the west of Montbéliard in front of the Belfort gap.

The French press on to the Vosges

The first plan conceived by General de Lattre de Tassigny, whose left flank reached Rupt-sur-Moselle at the end of September, was to force a way across the Vosges by the Col de la Schlucht. He was forced to change his mind, however, and accept Guebwiller as the initial objective for II Corps, which in a later phase of the battle thrust forward vigorously to reach the Rhine at Chalampé, thus pinning the left flank of the German 19th Army back on the Swiss frontier. With this aim, he reinforced General de Monsabert with three further divisions and the support of two others. Nevertheless the plan came to nothing, for two reasons. Firstly, while the French II Corps was struggling to reach the crest of the Vosges, the American 7th Army found itself drawn off in the divergent direction of the Saverne gap, and de Lattre was most reluctantly forced to use some of the troops he wanted to throw into attack for purposes of consolidation. Patch and Devers above him had simply acted in conformity with the instructions they received from S.H.A.E.F., namely to provide cover for the 12th Army Group (3rd Army) in its advance north-eastwards.

Secondly, the very heavy rains of autumn 1944 slowed down infantry, and blinded artillery and aircraft, with the added effect that as winter closed in and the men of II Corps scaled the long slopes of the Vosges, cases of frostbite grew numerous. The leather ankle-boot with its rubber sole was not the most successful article of American equipment.

Previous page: *French Moroccan goums move up behind the Colmar front.*
◁ ◁ *Infantry shelter in a depression in a wood before moving off into the attack.*
◁ *A Sherman covers a column of infantry moving up a country lane towards Metz.*
▽ *French spahis on forward reconnaissance. While two of them report by radio, the other two keep watch, fingers on the triggers of their machine guns.*

1944

June

15. U.S. 2nd and 4th Marine Divisions land on Saipan. First major air strike against Japan.
16. King George VI visits Normandy.
18. Russians pierce Mannerheim Line. U.S. forces cut off the Cherbourg peninsula.
20. Americans attack the outer defences of Cherbourg. 8th Army enters Perugia.
21. 1,000 bombers with escort of 1,200 fighters of the U.S.A.A.F. raid Berlin.
22. Break-out from Imphal after 88-day siege.
23. Channel storms abate and unloading recommences at "Mulberry" harbour.
25. Street fighting in Cherbourg. Vitebsk liberated.
26. Mogaung captured. British launch drive west of Caen.
27. Cherbourg taken.
28. British 2nd Army establishes bridgehead over Odon near Mondrainville.

July

2. Kluge takes over from Rundstedt.
3. Russians recapture Minsk.
4. British and Canadians take Carpiquet, west of Caen.
6. Churchill announces that 2,754 V-1's have caused 2,752 fatalities.
7. Japanese Admirals Nagumo and Yano killed in fighting on Saipan.
8. 2nd Army attacks Caen after the R.A.F. drops 2,500 tons of bombs.
9. Admiral Turner declares Saipan secure.
11. U.S. to recognise French Provisional Government.
12. Tactical Air Force attacks Po bridges. 5th Army reaches Lajatico.
13. 2nd Army takes Caen.
16. 8th Army takes Arezzo, reaches the Arno.
18. U.S. forces enter St Lô. 2nd Army launches "Goodwood". Tojo Cabinet resigns; Tojo replaced as Army chief by Umezu.

19. 2nd Army advances east of Caen. 5th Army takes Leghorn.
20. The July Bomb Plot. Attempted assassination of Hitler.
21. U.S. Marines land on Guam. Stulpnagel commits suicide.
24. U.S. Marines land on Tinian. Russians capture Maidenek concentration camp.
25. U.S. 1st Army launches "Cobra" breakout across Périers-St. Lô front, supported by 3,000 aircraft.
27. Breakout at St Lô.
30. 1st Army reaches Avranches. Russians establish bridgeheads over the Vistula.

August

1. Patton takes command of U.S. 3rd Army. Polish Home Army rises in Warsaw.
2. Tinian declared secure.
4. 8th Army reaches the outskirts of Florence. 3rd Army takes Rennes.
6. Nantes liberated. 3rd Army reaches outskirts of Brest. German counter-attack at Avranches.
8. Canadian 1st Army advances towards Falaise.
9. Eisenhower establishes H.Q. in France. U.S. 1st Army turns towards British to close Falaise gap.

10. Guam falls to 3rd Marine and 77th Divisions and 1st Marine Brigade.
11. Falaise gap reduced to 20 miles. 8th Army reaches Empoli.
12. "Pluto" pipeline begins operation between Isle of Wight and Cherbourg.
13. Allied bombers begins flying arms and ammunition to beleaguered Polish Home Army in Warsaw.
15. Operation "Anvil": U.S. and French forces invade southern France.
16. Me 163's attack B-17's for first time near Leipzig.
17. U.S. troops take St. Malo, Chartres, Orléans. Russians reach East Prussian border.
20. F.F.I. rises in Paris. U.S. 3rd Army establishes bridgehead over the Seine near Mantes-Gassincourt. Falaise pocket sealed off.
22. Fleet Air Arm begins attacks on the *Tirpitz* in Altenfjord.
23. F.F.I. takes over control of Paris. Allies take Grenoble and Marseilles.
25. Allied forces enter Paris.
27. Last Chindit units evacuated to India.

18. Germans counter-attack in Arnhem sectors. Brest capitulates.
19. U.S. and British troops meet at Nijmegen.
20. Finns and Russians sign provisional peace treaty. British and U.S. troops take Nijmegen bridges.
21. Polish parachute brigade lands in Arnhem area.
23. Dortmund-Ems canal breached in R.A.F. night raid.
25. Evacuation of surviving para-

28. Russians enter Transylvania. Last garrison in Marseilles surrenders, Toulon cleared of Germans.
30. Russians take Ploieşti.
31. British 2nd Army reaches Amiens, captures Somme bridge intact. 8th Army attacks on the Gothic Line. Russians take Bucharest. Montgomery promoted to Field-Marshal.

September

1. British enter Arras; Canadians take Dieppe, Rouen; Americans clear Verdun. 8th Army penetrates Montegridolfo position in the Gothic Line.
3. British 2nd Army liberates Brussels. French capture Lyons.
4. British 2nd Army liberates Antwerp.
5. Rundstedt appointed C.-in-C. West.
6. Home Guard training ended in Britain. Canadians invest Calais.
8. Russians enter Bulgaria unopposed. Bulgaria declares war on Germany. 5th Army begins large scale offensive on the Gothic Line. First V-2 lands in Chiswick, West London.
10. Russians capture Prague.
11. Second Quebec Conference begins. U.S. 1st Army patrol crosses German border near Stalzenburg.
12. German garrison in Le Havre surrenders.
14. Russians enter Warsaw suburb.
15. U.S. 1st Army breaches Siegfried Line. Marines land on Peleliu in Palaus. R.A.F. drops 12,000-lb bombs on *Tirpitz*.
16. End of the Second Quebec Conference.
17. Allied 1st Airborne Army lands in Holland near Eindhoven and Arnhem. Canadians begin six day battle for Boulogne.

troops at Arnhem begins. Hitler orders the formation of the *"Volkssturm"*.
26. 8th Army crosses the Rubicon.
30. Germans surrender in Calais.

October

2. Polish Home Army capitulates in Warsaw. R.A.F. breaches sea wall at Walcheren Island.
4. Operation "Manna": British forces land in Greece.
9. Third Moscow Conference.
10. Tank battle begins near Debrecen. Three Soviet corps destroyed.
12. British paratroops capture Athens airport.

13. Germans launch V-weapons against Antwerp. U.S. 1st Army enters Aix-la-Chapelle.
14. Athens cleared by the British. Rommel commits suicide.
16. Skorzenny kidnaps Nicholas Horthy, and forces Admiral Horthy to withdraw request for armistice.
18. Chiang Kai-shek demands Stilwell's resignation.
19. Moscow Conference ends. Hitler orders the destruction of Warsaw.
20. U.S. 6th Army invades Leyte.
22. Scheldt estuary cleared. Minesweeping operations begin.
23. Decisive Battle of Leyte Gulf starts.

25. Battle off Cape Engaño.
26. Leyte Gulf ends. Japanese lose four carriers and about 500 planes. Americans lose one light carrier and two escort carriers.
27. *Kamikaze* attacks on U.S. Task Force 38 in Phillipines. Canadians land on South Bevelland and link up with the British.
29. R.A.F. Lancasters bomb *Tirpitz* with 12,000-lb bombs.
30. Last gassing at Auschwitz.
31. R.A.F. Mosquitoes destroy Gestapo H.Q. at Aarhus.

November

1. Canadians land on Walcheren Island. Allies seize Westkapelle.
2. 14th Army takes Mawlu in Burma.
3. Allies occupy Flushing.
7. Roosevelt elected President for fourth term; Truman as Vice-President. Victor Sorge executed in Japan.
12. R.A.F. Lancasters sink the *Tirpitz* in Tromso Fjord.
18. U.S. 3rd Army crosses German frontier.
24. Allies cross the Saar, and French take Strasbourg. B-29's raid Tokyo from the Marianas for the first time.
25. U.S. troops break out of the Hurtgen forest. *Kamikaze* attacks on U.S. Navy near Luzon and in Leyte Gulf.
26. Port of Antwerp opened for shipping, but subject to V-1 and V-2 attacks.
27. Cordell Hull resigns; Edward Stettinius nominated as U.S. Secretary of State.

December

2. De Gaulle arrives in Moscow for talks with Stalin.
3. Home Guard stands down in Britain.
4. Athens under martial law after riots.
7. U.S. troops land near Ormoc on Leyte island.
8. U.S.A.A.F. begins 72-day bombardment of Iwo Jima.
10. 14th Army reaches Indaw.
12. 8th Army establishes bridgehead across the Naviglio Canal. U.S. troops capture V-weapon plant at Wittring.
13. 7th Army captures Niederroedern. 3rd Army captures Metz.